A Story for Every Day of SUMMER

Edited by John Howes and Fran Neatherway

First Printing, 2023

ISBN: 9798387153044
Imprint: Independently published

For more information about The Cafe Writers of Rugby,
visit their website, www.rugbycafewriters.com

Dedication

This book is dedicated to our dear friends
Christine Hancock and Peter Maudsley,
members of the Rugby Cafe Writers,
both no longer with us,
but remembered with great affection.
May the stories never end.

A Story for Every Day of Summer

Introduction: Who are the Cafe Writers?

Does everyone secretly want to be a great writer? Maybe not everyone but who would not jump at the chance to have an article, a story, a poem or even a book published in their own name?

I worked for 25 years as a journalist on local newspapers and I can remember the thrill of seeing my name in the *Rugby Advertiser* for the first time. Not, fortunately, in the court reports, but as the author of a couple of articles in my very first edition as a junior reporter. "By John Howes" it said under the stories. I carefully cut them out and pasted them into my scrapbook which I still have and glance at occasionally. I had written something of value, something which other people might like to read. Several decades later, I get a similar, if not quite so exciting, feeling when I see my name in print, whether it is an article in the parish magazine or one of my poems or stories in a published anthology. I have created something and perhaps - just perhaps - someone else might take a look at it.

Some of the writers in this collection are very used to seeing their name displayed publicly. Some are professional writers and will often glance along the bookshop or supermarket shelves to see one of their titles staring back at them. But for others, this may be the first time their work has been published in a real book, on sale, for the public to buy. Imagine how exciting this must be for them - a physical object (or even an ebook!) to send off to friends and family. It's a permanent reminder of something they have created; something for future generations to look at and enjoy.

That is the great joy of being part of the Rugby Cafe Writers. We were created about five years ago by Theresa Le Flem, a romantic novelist and inspiration to many of us. She called together a group of people who enjoyed writing and who loved books.

We always welcome new members but find some a bit reticent. They say, "I have never had anything published. I couldn't possibly read anything out loud." This is perfectly understandable but I always say, "Don't worry. We have all been there. We all think, at some stage, that we are not good enough." But we encourage each other, offer support and make suggestions in the kindest of ways and we have seen many members gain confidence and look forward to sharing their work with others in the group.

In this anthology - the third we have published in the past five years - you will find a selection of short stories, one to read for each day of summer. They are all quick reads and shouldn't take you more than five minutes. They are not all on the subject of summer but hopefully you will find them entertaining, relaxing and, on occasion, moving - and wherever you are this summer, we hope you will be able to sit back with our anthology, de-stress and enjoy the book.

John Howes
www.rugbycafewriters.com

Contents

A Story for Every Day of Summer

A Story for Every Day of Summer

June 1: Detective

"It's a good story, but I don't believe a word of it," Bernard said. He stood tall, hands on hips, glaring at his five employees.

They should have been laughing. It was utterly ridiculous. But Bernard's stern nature always left them fearful.

"Stains do not magically appear on kitchen floors," he argued. "We are the only people in this building, and I know I didn't throw my lunch around. That means it's one of you."

Bernard's recent binge-fest of *Poirot* had seeped into his soul. He was riding high on the thrill of playing detective, even if it was to the world's most pathetic crime. He paced up and down the small office, his hand under his chin in a melodramatic thinking pose.

"I know who did it," he announced, turning to face his suspects. "I'm going to give you one more chance to confess. Confess and the punishment will be lenient."

He hadn't yet decided what punishment was suitable for someone spilling soup on the floor and not mopping it up, but he had time to think of something fitting.

No one said a word. The tension was rising. Bernard imagined that the perpetrator was writhing with guilt. It was lost on him that his staff were gobsmacked at how ridiculous he was being.

"Carla," he said, pointing a finger directly at the young woman. "It wasn't you. I know this as it was chicken soup and you're a vegan."

Carla glanced at her colleagues. Bernard saw relief in her eyes. It was actually disbelief.

"Becky," he said next, his finger moving on. "Your breath stinks of onions. It wasn't you." Becky closed her mouth tightly.

"So, it's one of you men," Bernard accused, hands back on his hips. "And I know which one."

The men were utterly speechless. After a dramatic pause, the sort that Agatha Christie herself would have been proud of, Bernard declared, "It was you, Archie. You are the chicken soup spiller. And do you know how I know?"

Archie shook his head. He really wasn't bothered.

"Because you've also spilt some on your tie."

Lindsay Woodward

June 2: The Chauffeur

In the final year of his working life, my ex-father-in-law was chauffeur to an old lady who lived in a rotting pile on a run-down estate in Shropshire.

His duties were light, as she rarely left the house, so he occupied his time in keeping the car in immaculate condition.

"When I die, I'll leave you the Rolls," she said.

He was allocated a dismal, basement flat, particularly gloomy on a dark, dank November afternoon. There was a sparsely furnished living room, a rudimentary kitchen and a tiny scullery, housing a coal-fired copper wash-boiler. Above the living room was a large bedroom, with a double bed which had seen better days.

He would have gone slowly demented had it not been for Kim. She was a golden retriever, a quiet and doting best friend, who listened to his every word, ears cocked, as she gazed at him with her soulful eyes. She followed her master everywhere, resting her head on his feet as he sat on the old leather armchair in the evening, and sleeping on the threadbare rug at the end of his bed at night.

One dark morning, between sleeping and waking, my father-in-law had the alarming sensation that someone had their hands tightly round his throat. He woke to see a woman, with red hair and a ruddy face, looking down at him in utter amazement. She wore an old blue gabardine coat, and a red beret pulled down onto her ears.

He croaked a scream for Kim, but there was no response. Throwing on his clothes, he went down the stairs to find Kim quaking at the bottom. In the storeroom, boxes of washing powder were scattered on the floor. Kim could not have reached the shelf.

Kim at his heels, he went into the stable yard. The estate workers were having their tea break. He engaged them in casual conversation.

"Who lived in the flat before me?"

"The previous chauffeur lived there, but his wife died and he left soon after."

"What was she like?"

"Oh, a big woman, red in the face, a real battleaxe. Always wore an old blue coat down to her ankles and a red beret pulled down over her ears. She ruled the roost there all right."

My father-in-law gave in his notice soon after that. He never did get the Rolls.

Wendy Goulstone

June 3: Scarborough Fair

It was years since I had been to the annual local fair. In fact it must have been at least forty years since I last wandered through the stalls with their offerings, mostly homemade but seen through my teenage eyes and a little blinded with first love. Memories rushed in and I felt again the thrill of questioning my love.

I wondered if anyone from that time was here today. I started looking at the faces, looking for a familiar face just in case. Then all of a sudden there she was. The years had been gentle to her, and I remembered her beautiful eyes. Why, oh why, had I left the next day and not returned? Would she recognize me? Dare I remind her of that last day or would she be offended after all these years?

As my memories flooded back I decided I would be very careful with my response (just in case she didn't remember the last time we were together).

"After all these years to meet like this at the fair. Have you been here all the time or are you visiting like me?"

"I live here, I've made my life here as I had some tasks to complete, I was asked to make a shirt and find an acre of land between the salt water and the sea strands."

She hadn't even stopped to think, her memory was as strong as mine. I had asked for those plus much, much more.

I found myself saying: "I too had looked for the land between the salt water and the sea strands. I had found it."

I just stood there looking at her and not knowing what to say. She smiled and everything was as if we were picking up where we left forty years ago. For she once was a true love of mine.

Pam Barton

June 4: The 'B' Road

It was late, the road was dark. The van was heavy-laden with props. We were heading back to London after a successful tour of the North.

Then we hit fog. Thick incandescent fog that wrapped itself around us, obscured the road and made the windscreen wipers scream in pain as they smeared across our vision.

And then Fiona did a curious thing. Fiona was the Stage Manager and she was driving. I was more than happy to let her drive, until now.

In the densest of fogs she accelerated. At great speed.

I was petrified. This defied all logic and the natural human instinct for survival. But I couldn't dissuade her.

"If we hit anything at all it will be over quickly, so why worry? Besides, I want to get home."

This was a side I hadn't seen previously; until that point she had been the steady cautious, punctilious manager of props and costumes and script that all of her breed are. Not very exciting, not very imaginative but steady. And then the needle was on red.

It was an old Ford Transit van, bought with the last of our Arts Council Grant and I had no idea how much fuel the empty tank might hold. But I knew slowing down might help us. But Fiona? Undaunted, she pushed her foot to the floor and we careered around corners dangerously overweight.

It was like being at sea in a storm. And then we saw it like an oasis in the darkness: a succession of bright neon lights and an illuminated shop front. A solitary rust-coloured pump standing in the forecourt. We slowed to a halt with a sudden lurch.

A group of men sat huddled inside the building swathed in steam.

The look of desperation and despair must have been apparent as we entered the billowing warmth inside.

Sullen faces scared from knife fights stared at us in silence.

"Excuse me," I said in a high contralto voice. "But do you have any petrol?"

And then they fell about laughing.

Simon Grenville

June 5: Silver Jubilee, Malta, 1977

I remember when it was June 5th 1977, the day of the Silver Jubilee celebrations. We - husband Peter and our two small sons, Tony, three and Chris, a toddling one-year-old - were in Malta on a two-year Married Accompanied posting.

It was 45 years ago when we woke certain it would be a fabulously sunny, hot, Maltese day for the celebration barbecue. There wasn't any rain to dampen proceedings; we hadn't had rain for months.

Preparations began early in Egmont Close, our concrete built apartments known as 'Colditz' after the Prisoner of War camp in World War Two. The buildings were brightened with flags of many countries. Outside, the buildings were cold, uninspiring, without kerb appeal. However, inside, the rooms were spacious, four bedrooms and a long hall for the children to safely ride their tricycles.

We brought our own steak, beef burgers and sausages for the barbecue, with coleslaw and salads provided. The drink we took included crates of beer; Hop Leaf, Cisk and Blue with very cheap Marsovin Maltese wine from the farm shop with painful hangovers suffered the following day.

All the children were in fancy dress. There were pirates, nurses, witches, clowns, the King of Hearts and an older child was dressed as a baby with dummy in his mouth and a sun hat as he sat in a baby's push-chair. I dressed the boys simply in the heat. Tony was an Austrian boy in shorts with braces, shirt and an Austrian-style hat. Chris was dressed as Tarzan toddling around centre stage in his one-sided towelling brown and blue swimsuit.

Everyone seemed to enjoy themselves. The Admiral, Oswald Nigel Amherst Cecil, and his wife attended and gave prizes to competition winners. Peter won the crate of beer race; however the beer was drunk on each lap of the course and the prize, a crate of 24 bottles, had been drunk. He returned the empties to the local Briffa brothers' shop where he received a penny a bottle for recycling! A great time was had by all with noisy festivities continuing long into the night. **Kate A.Harris**

June 6: Never Before! Never Again?

"Bored! Bored! Bored!" she exclaimed, as they lay in bed on that fateful Saturday morning, enjoying a leisurely breakfast.

"Did you know," he said, leafing through *The Economist*, "there are 8,780 communes in France with less than 200 inhabitants each?"

"Didn't you hear me?" she said. "I'm BORED! We never do anything new anymore and I'm BORED!"

"What exactly are you bored with, darling?" he said. "Are you tired of this brand of marmalade, or do you want to buy a big yacht and sail around the world? Where exactly are you on the marmalade-yacht boredom continuum?"

"Oh I don't know." she said. "It's definitely more than marmalade, but less than yacht. I think. We used to be wacky and exciting. Now we're respectable and BORING!"

"OK," he said, realising that this couldn't be batted away with more coffee and amazing facts from *The Economist*, "let's go away for a weekend and do something new, like hot-air ballooning."

"We did that once, and it crashed!" she said. "Darling, that's how hot-air balloons land!" He explained. She wasn't amused. She hadn't been at the time either.

One week later, she found herself dressed like a trainee astronaut, strapped to a guy half her age, communicating by sign on account of being at 12,000 feet in a light aircraft with the door open. The guy, in turn, was attached to a large parachute. A green light flickered on the ceiling of the aircraft. In one movement, they tumbled out into free space.

He was waiting below, filming the tandem freefall parachute drop. "That looks exciting, but rather her than me," he thought.

On the back seat of their car lay a beautifully wrapped package. It contained three of the most expensive jars of marmalade he could find.

Simon Parker

June 7: Time To Leave

Sitting with his feet in the water, Jacob hoped the rising tide wouldn't totally cover the lower platform on the jetty. He didn't really want to move. Not just yet. He played idly with the weight on the wound-up crabbing line, avoiding the barbed points on the two hooks. Next to his bucket was a large piece of suet, bait for the crabs that clustered on the sand around the piling.

He could feel the waves tapping beneath him on the underside of the platform. There was still more than an hour to go until high tide; the platform would be under water for definite. Wiping his face, Jacob hauled himself to his feet, dropped the crabline into the green plastic bucket, and climbed the half dozen steps to the main platform. Mercifully, the only other people on the jetty, three fishermen sharing a flask of coffee and 'one that got away' tales, were well away from the exit bridge.

Jacob left the jetty and headed for his car. The cry of a seagull, on the wind, sounded like a child's cry, and for a moment Jacob froze, and his heart stopped. He started to say 'Benny?' before he could stop himself. Shaking his head, he gently placed Ben's bucket into the boot of the car, then sat behind the wheel, watching the sea creep up the sand, and the families leaving the beach, probably to get ice-creams or fizzy drinks before returning to their caravans or rented cottages.

He dropped his forehead onto the steering wheel. He waited.

It was dark when he turned the key in the ignition, put his foot on the accelerator, revved the engine, and surged forward over the sand, racing into the deep water.

"I'm so sorry, Benny," he said quietly, as the water rushed in through the open windows.

EE Blythe

June 8: Escape

The arch loomed in front of her. It was dark and forbidding, but the only way out. She pushed open the wooden door, stepped into a gloomy tunnel and ran, splashing through foetid puddles, trying not to slip on the slimy ground. There was no sound of pursuit, but she knew they were still behind her. She could almost smell them.

The giant Hounds and their Masters never gave up. They captured their quarry or died in the attempt. Footsteps and voices echoed through the passages. They were getting closer. Angered by her escape, they would not be gentle with her – if their employer still wanted her taken alive. If not, she'd heard stories of what they did to their prey.

She saw a patch of blackness on her left and without hesitation swerved into a side tunnel. It petered out. For a moment she thought she'd run into a trap. Then she saw a faint light above. She'd found one of the shafts leading to the surface. A ladder was fixed to the wall and broken off just out of her reach. Somehow she leapt up and caught the bottom rung. The ladder creaked and swayed, scattering flakes of rust as she scrambled towards safety. With one last burst of strength, she shoved aside the metal grill blocking her exit.

And something grabbed her. A talon-like hand was gripping her ankle, yellow nails digging into her. She kicked hard, managing to shake it off. The man dropped down the shaft, screaming, and landed with a thump.

She hoped he had been alone. She couldn't hear any sounds of pursuit as she lay at the top of the shaft, panting. There was no time to rest. She had to move onwards.

Her muscles strained as she dragged the metal grill back over the shaft. It wouldn't hold the Hound Masters for long, but it might give her the time to escape. Her leg was throbbing where the hunter had grabbed it. Should she run or hide? The Hounds could easily outrun her and they would scent her if she hid. Best to hide while she rested her painful ankle and wait for daybreak when the Hounds were weakened by the sun.

She limped through the darkness, listening for the sounds of pursuit behind her. The empty streets were full of rubble, making them difficult to traverse safely. She looked for a safe hiding place and spotted a tall tower. If the stairs were intact, she could reach the top and block the stairwell.

She was in luck. The narrow spiral staircase wound its way upwards into the gloom. Not having the time, or the strength, to block the entrance, she hobbled up the stairs. Perhaps the Hounds would search the lower floors first.

Time was running out. She forced her tired body to climb the steep steeps to the roof. A wooden trapdoor was the next obstacle to be faced, but it opened easily and she emerged onto the battlements. The devastated city spread out below her, scarred by flames, its buildings destroyed in earlier attacks.

She slammed the trapdoor shut and looked for something to keep it closed. There was nothing, no lock, no bolt. Only her. What as she going to do? She needed to think, but she was interrupted by a loud voice echoing across the sky.

"Turn that thing off and go to sleep. You've got school in the morning. Have you done your homework?"

With a sigh, Daisy closed her laptop. "Yes, Mum."

Fran Neatherway

June 9: The removal gang

When her mother died, Gwendoline inherited the lot. And she hated it all.

The cat purring, seeking attention in front of the dormant electric fire. The radiogram broadcasting the Home Service - Forces Favourites. Warming on the table, the pot of tea, the rock cakes and the neatly-cut sandwiches. Thick net curtains shielding the room from passing glances. Everywhere there were things: nick-nacks, ornaments, family photographs, and mementoes of dismal holidays. It was hard to breathe in that room. Afternoon light disappeared and the standard lamp shone bright, but not bright enough for the dingy corners. The room seemed to wait expectantly for the visitor who never came.

Precisely one day after mother was safely encased underground, Gwendoline put away her mourning clothes and returned to real life. After all, this was the 1960s and she was a woman on the way up. There was no better personal assistant than her. She dressed smartly and acted even smarter. Gwendoline had reddish neatly-cropped hair, piercing blue eyes and tidy lips. She stood out in a crowd of nonentities and kept herself aloof from admiring glances.

Her clothes were simple but clinical, well-contrasted colours and finished off by a blue necklace which she had bought herself. She was 32 and single; her expression was consistently serious and her emotions, if she had any, were kept well-hidden. Her impressively tidy desk suggested everything in her life had its place and she exercised total control over it.

Beneath the surface, it was another story. There was something wild waiting to get out.

The van arrived shortly after 8am.

"Everything," she told the two overalled shifters.

"Everything?" queried Sid, or whatever he was called.

"Everything," she repeated, leading them into the front room to begin the clearance.

It took roughly two hours to finish the "lounge" as her mother had called it. There were so many items to wrap for the auction. The three-piece suite drew admiring glances from Alf, the other shifter.

Murphy the cat looked on quizzically. He sat in a corner, occasionally cleaning his black and grey coat. His tail shot up with a question every now and then. Not the comfy chair, surely. Once he leapt up and sprang on to the remaining armchair, thinking this might prevent its journey to the auction. But the shifters shook him off and shooed him back into the corner.

Gwendoline did little. She certainly didn't make the boys a cuppa, and there was no way she was going to enter into a conversation. What on earth would they talk about? The football results?

She took the opportunity to oversee the installation of a telephone line. She disliked intrusion intensely and, if she could combine the visits of workmen into one long morning, that would be considered a good result. Just for good measure, at lunchtime some new pieces would be arriving. 'Contemporary' might be a good description - a sofa which looked glorious, though was a little upright to relax on , a standard lamp straight out of a magazine and the very latest hi-fi for her Andy Williams collection.

"It's all gone, miss," said Sid, interrupting her at the dining table, and casting a lecherous glance towards her neat curves.

"Thank you," replied Gwendoline.

"We found this, though," added Sid, producing an old green wooden box from behind his back. "Behind the old sofa, tucked away".

The box, just a few inches long, had a hinged lid. The surface was smooth but dappled in places. There was a fastener but no lock. Once, it could have held letters tied up with ribbons but now it was empty. Its secrets had fled.

Gwendoline stole a glance at it. She hesitated.

"Take that, as well. Take the bloody lot," she said finally.

"As you wish, madam," said Sid who then departed.

The box was uncomfortable for Gwendoline. When she was a child, so young and so carefree, she'd kept her imaginary dreams in it. Everytime life became hard, she would retreat to open the box and retrieve a hope for the future - a make-believe ballet shoe, a giant seashell, a train ticket to Baghdad, silk from her Bedouin tent, ice still unmelted from her Arctic hut. Every dream was there. Every fantasy unfulfilled because of her. Her mother.

And now mother and her porcelain collection were gone, life was about to start - for real. There were going to be some changes around here.

John Howes

June 10: New arrivals

Yesterday, the Ferrari had been unloaded at Tilbury docks. It had been in a container shipped from New York. The bright red racer had crossed the Atlantic to be with the Vincetti family. It had journeyed directly to the New York boulevards.

Now, it was en route to Bedford; attracting many stares and lustful nods from motorists and pedestrians alike. It almost caused an accident outside the recently opened pet shop. Gemma was so excited. Her uncle had promised her a new car, but this!

Her father, Gerraldo, popped the bonnet. His face filled with fear. There had been castaways. Twenty strings were swaying in the breeze. There was no breeze. The threads were hundreds of tiny spiders awakening in the cool Spring air.

Arturo closed the bonnet quietly.

"We need to call the Environmental Health Department."

In less than half an hour, Adrian Hunter turned up. He inspected the new arrivals.

With eyes behind pebble glasses, he whispered, "Lucky you rang. These are poisonous. They are called the Brown Recluse."

Then he brightened. "I'll give them a good home. I'll include them in my school visit tour of the home counties. Thank you. Give me an hour before you come out of your house. Bye."

Arturo wiped his brow. "Close call. He's got the right name, hasn't he?"

"Yes, I'm going to call her Bella." They both shivered as they looked at the car number plate. BEL written in red.

"Glad you didn't call her Christine. That would be too much."

Paul Clark

June 11: Imprisoned

Denis opened his eyes and sat up. Had he been asleep? Where was he? It was surprisingly dark. There was little difference to having his eyes open or closed. He blinked a couple of times just to prove it to himself. He'd been there a while although he couldn't be sure exactly how long.

He heard voices shouting in the distance and he called to them, but nobody came. The floor was hard and cool to the touch. He ran his fingers over it, and something pricked his finger, he guessed he was sitting on bare floorboards.

He looked around, there was a thin slice of light creeping underneath a door. A door - that was an obvious way out. Denis suspected his captors had secured it but it made sense to check it anyway. He crawled closer and felt over its surface, searching for a handle. There was nothing. He put his shoulder to it and shoved but it wouldn't budge. His eyes were becoming accustomed to the lack of light, so he decided to investigate the small space in which he found himself imprisoned.

He reached above him, there wasn't enough space to stand up. His poor old knees creaked as he crawled over to the furthest wall. Feeling his way with his hands, he touched feathers and immediately recoiled. Denis had a bit of a phobia about birds at the best of times and to find a dead one as his cellmate was the stuff of nightmares. He shuffled away in reverse and bumped into something. On inspection he found it was a cardboard box. He felt inside and picked up one of the cold, oddly textured cylinders he found there. When he found the piece of thread at one end he thought it might be dynamite but then decided that a candle was more likely. The box was full of them, all different sizes. Despite searching there were no matches.

His mouth was dry, he needed a drink. He'd love a cup of tea but that wasn't very likely. How had he managed to get himself into this situation? He tried to remember but that was no longer one of his strong points. He shoved the box in frustration and some things clattered to the floor.

After some tactile identification, he discovered he now had what he thought were a tea tray, some cloths, a pencil and a small piece of plastic that may have been a credit card, but Denis couldn't be sure. More worryingly, there was some sort of chain. He didn't like the feel of the cold links running through his fingers and he quickly put it down. He didn't want to think too much about the sort of people who had put him in here. He needed to concentrate on escaping.

I'm getting out of here, he thought. He crawled back to the door pushing his treasure in front of him on the tray. He jammed the plastic card in the edge of the door near the latch, he placed the tea tray on the pencil to create a see-saw effect and slid it half under the door. He knelt on the other end of the tray to provide some leverage. After applying some force it shifted and with a click the door opened and light flooded in. He blinked at the brightness. Denis stared out for a moment and took in the unfamiliar space: a narrow corridor with terracotta floor tiles and high skirting boards. Where on earth was he? He inched out onto the tiled floor and, after a few attempts, stood up slowly. What now? It was still quiet apart from the distant hum of a television. Were his captors nearby? His heart started to race.

He looked both ways down the corridor. Closed doors at both ends. One was solid wood, the other had an ornate stained glass panel. There were birds in the panel – he didn't like birds. Suddenly the door opened and a woman came inside bringing the chill of winter with her.

"Are you OK?" she asked.

"I was trapped in there with a dead bird!" he said pointing behind him.

She chuckled. "No, that's a feather duster, we keep bits and pieces in that cupboard. Ooh look there's the dog's spare choke chain." She shut the door and turned her attention back to Denis. "I did warn you not to play hide and seek with the grandchildren, now didn't I, Dad?"

Bella Osborne .

June 12: The Room And The View

The commissar was in a terrible mood; perhaps Prisoner Six might yield better results. He gazed out of the window, open to allow the smell of grass cuttings and the scraping sound of masonry trowels to enter the bright room. There was a wooden chair that could be easily turned from one interrogator to the next.

Outside, he could see students walking across the ornately statued square that dated back to Napoleonic times, now damaged by mortar fire. The lieutenants dragged in a tall man with wavy black hair and a large nose, already bruised around the temples, and roughly flung him down.

"No. Not there. Bring him much nearer the window."

The hedge trimmer was audible to the new victim.

"We haven't had much luck with your comrades. They have filled our body bags so let's try a different game. You tell me where the president is hiding and not only will you go free but but all these people will be safe."

He pulled out a Makarov pistol and shot a gardener in the chest.

"Monster! They have done exactly nothing wrong!"

"What about that pretty student in the yellow coat, comrade? I can just about hit her from here."

Suddenly, Prisoner Six jumped head first out of the window. The 'dead' gardener jumped up and with his team grabbed the dust sheet containing the hedge cuttings forming a crashmat for the four-storey drop. The pretty girl in the yellow coat produced a Kalashnikov from a fake statue and laid down suppressing fire. The commissar and the lieutenants could do little. Then silence and an empty square.

Later, in the park, Prisoner Six asked the yellow coat girl, "Commander. Still three to get out. Has my brother sent other Units?"

"Don't worry. The president will soon set the whole country free," she said.

Chris Wright

June 13: A First Time For Everything

Only one go at this, no second chances. There were others present, but they couldn't hear. The conversation was going on in his head.

Could be worse, I'm pretty comfortable. Better than a few weeks ago. But then, I didn't expect to try this out.

A distant voice said something about 'rambling on', but what he was saying was clear enough in his head; he was trying out something new... new to him anyway, and he was going to make the best of it.

'Fresh as a Daisy', that's a saying isn't it. Quite appropriate really, they talk about pushing up daisies.

The distant voice said, "He's talking about flowers, I think." A familiar woman's voice this time.

She's right too, he thought, she'd been right about most things over the years. He'd be one up now though, she certainly hadn't tried this one.

Pity there won't be a mobile connection. I could tell her all about it.

"I think he's on about his mobile."

Once muffled voices were clearer now, although he couldn't hear them.

"We'll never know; he's gone. At least it was peaceful."

David J Boulton

June 14: Not So Sleepy Beauty

Once upon a time, in a country far, far away there lived a good King and his Queen. Together they were wise and kind and ruled a fair and just kingdom. Their lives were full and happy, except for one thing - although they dearly wished for it, they had no children.

Many years passed and then one day, the queen had some happy tidings and nine months later gave birth to a lovely, healthy baby girl. The King and Queen were delighted and the whole kingdom rejoiced.

The King and Queen threw a grand celebration and invited everyone they could think of including all the fairies in the kingdom. But in the midst of everything, they forgot to invite one old fairy who lived at the edge of the forest. When the old fairy heard that she was the only one in the kingdom not to receive an invitation, she became enraged and, with an evil plan in her mind, decided to go to the celebrations anyway.

When it was time to gift the baby with special wishes, the good fairies wished her well and said, "May she grow to be the most beautiful girl in the world! She will sing sweetly and dance so well! She will live happily!" All the fairies blessed the young princess and gave her beautiful gifts.

But, when it was the old fairy's turn, she cursed her instead. "On this baby's sixteenth birthday she will touch a spindle, and die!"

The King and Queen were shocked. At first they didn't believe that anyone could wish such a thing on an innocent baby, but when they realised how angry and bitter the old fairy was they became afraid. They begged the old fairy to forgive them and take back her words, but the fairy refused to do so and left.

The other fairies were beside themselves. The old fairy's magic was much stronger than all of theirs combined, but they were heartbroken at the King and Queen's grief and came up with a plan.

"We cannot undo what the old fairy has spoken. But we certainly can make it different. Your child shall not die when she touches the spindle. But she will fall into a deep sleep for a hundred years. Then, a prince will come along and wake her up."

This wasn't perfect but it was better than death. The King and the Queen were relieved and a thought was planted in their heads – make it different!

As their daughter grew the King and Queen educated her well, not just about running a kingdom and being a princess, but also all about the old fairy's curse. They taught her how to use a spinning wheel properly and what a spindle was. The good fairies' bending of the curse was a good thing but they would prefer for it not to happen at all.

The princess grew up to be a kind and thoughtful girl who helped people in need and was a joy to be around. Everybody loved her. The years passed quickly, as they do, and soon it was the princesses sixteenth birthday.

She was taking her usual walk in the woods when she saw an old lady spinning. She knew at once who it was, for her parents had taught her well and why would an old lady be spinning in the middle of the woods?

She waved to the woman and continued on her way, ignoring the old lady's calls to come closer. When she arrived back at the castle, there was a spindle lying on the floor of her bedroom. The princess smiled at the old fairy's cleverness as she called a servant to take it away. Her sixteenth birthday passed as gloriously as all the ones before it and the curse was broken.

Hiding from the spinning wheels doesn't work.

Terri Brown

June 15: Bert Scoggins

The name's Scoggins. Bert Scoggins.

What's that? You want to know how the Folk Club's finances stay afloat?

Well, it's due to something that happened three years ago....

Somebody, I don't remember who, discovered that the American Pete Seeger was going to visit Britain and managed to book him. I wasn't initially impressed when he turned up with what looked like an outsize banjo, but he was friendly enough and chatted to some of the people in the front row while waiting to start.

The Corn Exchange was packed. I realised then that with all the entrance money the club's financial problems were over.

Pete Seeger's performance was very well received, especially his numbers such as *Jimmy Crack Corn* and *Red River Valley*. At one point he produced a lump of wood and an axe, and chopped the wood rhythmically while singing. Chips of wood flew everywhere but the audience loved it.

I wasn't so pleased because I knew who was going to have to clear up the mess.

After the concert he stayed behind to chat. I can't remember many people asking for an autograph, though. Some of them went off to the Eagle and suggested he might join them.

After thanking us for the chance to perform, he carefully picked up his banjo. Without a sound, he turned around and walked away.

Jim Hicks

June 16: What Is In The Box?

Having ransacked every drawer in the house we accepted the fact that the key was well and truly lost. So we perched on the edge of tea chests hugging mugs of tea. None of us had seen the box before, but then, mother was always somewhat secretive.

When we were children she used to slip out without saying where she was going, disappear until tea- time, then come back flustered, red in the face, and flap around in the kitchen, rattling pans.

"Probably love letters," said my sister, ever the romantic.

"Whose?" said my brother.

"Not Dad's," we said in unison.

Dad wasn't that sort. I never saw him kiss our mother or call her by anything other than her name. He never remembered her birthday; never gave her a Christmas present. How can you forget Christmas? And as for flowers, we had given up on dropping hints about that, years ago.

"Let's prise it open," said my sister, the practical one. "Anyone got a knife?"

No-one had, and Mum's knives were packed in the depths of a crate, until some day in the future when we would have time to unpack and share the contents of our parents' home.

"A hairpin! Who has a hairpin?" My brother's bright idea. But, of course, no-one had.

So we put the box on the window sill and went back up to finish clearing the attic, where we found a shoebox tied with ribbon, in which, lying under a pile of Mum's diaries, we found a small, tarnished key.

Back downstairs we stared at the box, speechless for once, torn between curiosity and fear.

"Open it."

The key shook in my hands as I fumbled for the keyhole. Inside lay a bundle of letters, faded, fragile, tied with a ribbon, each beginning 'My Darling', each ending with a row of kisses, but no name. Except for the last, which read: 'Are you sure? Have you been to the doctor? I can't leave her. She's ill. Look, I can't cope with this."

But no name. No kisses.

"What date does it say?"

But there were no dates, no envelopes, no postmarks. We looked at each other. Which of us?

Wendy Goulstone

June 17: In The Shoe Shop

Stacey snoozed her alarm, several times, until she could snooze it no more. She had calculated the precise number of minutes it would take her to get dressed and walk to the shopping mall in the summer sunshine, arriving exactly on time - but no earlier - than was absolutely necessary.

This wasn't what Stacey wanted to do. She worked in Bargain Shoes, a strip-light beacon of doom in the windowless precinct, stacked high with cheapness, bad designer-label copies and the occasional customer desperate to spend less than twenty quid.

She'd been there since finishing her college course in public service: her dream of being a police officer, or more precisely a detective, lying in tatters after her lack of attendance had resulted in a less than impressive end-of-year report.

Stacey was a trainee shop assistant with no knowledge or interest in shoes, yet she was often left in charge of the store. Every day was a drudge, and she'd lost count of the number of times she eyed the clock.

That morning, David walked in, early, mid-forties, maybe. Ordinary looking, could be worse. After mooching about for a while, he plonked a pair of trainers on the counter.

"Nineteen ninety-nine," she said, robotically.

"Thanks," he replied, and, after a pause, "How are you today?"

She was somewhat taken aback. Nobody asked her this, ever. She was nobody in a nothing shop, plying crap to cheapskates.

Stacey glanced at David. Their eyes didn't quite meet. Momentarily, she imagined rolling under the covers with him, exchanging secrets, making plans. But when she looked up, he was reaching for his credit card, ready to make a quick exit.

"I'm okay," she lied.

Without a sound, he turned around and walked away.

John Howes

June 18: Orange

Nadia held the orange closer to get a better look. She held it farther away, in case she was missing something. She smelled it, and unsurprisingly, it smelled like an orange, combined with a tinge of the perfume she wore on her wrist. She gave up on the orange and took another look at the note that had been pinned to it: "I saw this and thought of you."

This was not what she had expected to find when she had returned to her computer at reception, nor was the sentiment one that she had expected to find attached to an unassuming piece of citrus. She turned the note over in case she had missed something. Nothing.

She never wore orange nail polish, or eye shadow, or much of anything orange at all. She couldn't recall eating one in public recently. It was not a fruit or colour she thought about often. She continued to think about the orange and the note as she checked books out to a tired looking college student. She thought about who had come into the library that day. Had the coworker left the orange? If so, why wouldn't they just hand it to her?

Was it an insult, or a compliment? If it had been a peach, she might have been offended. If it were a lime or dragon fruit, she might have been flattered. But an orange was just an orange.

While she was thinking, a regular came up to the desk with his latest stack of overdue books. Nadia had always thought he was both incredibly handsome and irritating, since he always brought back his books at least two weeks late. If it weren't for his terrible borrowing habits, she probably would have asked him out. He seemed to like her as well.

"Hi," he said, placing the books on the counter.

"Hello," Nadia replied absent-mindedly. From her face he could tell she was deep in thought about something else.

"What's the matter," he said. "Orange you glad to see me?"

Holland Guthrie

June 19: Opera Outdoors

This bloody wind! Can't get me fag lit a' all.

- Here, let me help-a.

A flashy lighter suddenly appears about ten centimetres from me face. Flashy lighter from a flashy-lookin' bloke. God! What a creep he looks. Covered in bling – and old and paunchy, but not one to miss an opportunity, obviously. He's grabbed me effin' hand! I draw on the fag. If he gets too close I'll blow out my thanks to him right into his old wrinkly, flabby face.

But his windshield worked, and he's stepped back.

- My pleasure, I hear in a posh but foreign accent. I nod my thanks and blow the smoke away from him.

- You are relaxing before your performance?

- Er, yeh, I say.

- Isa not good for your voice, or for you. It will ruin your looks, and your health-a, as well. And you 'ava great voice, full of promise, and looks, and health, and youtha, but wait. One you will definitely lose with time, but don't lose the others too soon, my dear.

He bows. Definitely a foreigner. I smile, and he turns to go. I bet he'll strut, but I then I suddenly stop him –

- Why've you come here? To opera in the open-air? I ask.

-Is-a my job.

- Huh?

- I'm the conductor. Make sure your voice makes a good job-a of your aria, my dear. And (his podgy finger waves in my face) give up smoking.

And he turns a body, well-coordinated beneath the flab and off he does strut, confident and swift. And I'm left wishing he'd stayed. I fling the ciggy onto the grass. No more fags, I vow. I stamp my resolution out on it. I'll sing my heart out for you, I vow. And I do.

Chris Rowe

June 20: The Great Rug Of Rugby

The Bayeux Tapestry? Yes, we all know about that, but the Great Rug of Rugby? Maybe just a few bearded scholars at Warwick University value its worth and treasure its history but, apart from that, it is largely unknown. In hope of its worth being more widely recognized, a few precious snippets were presented to the V and A at the end of the 1920s but nothing came of it and all was promptly forgotten. So much for London's view of the Midlands.

Should you wish to see this great treasure yourself, then make your way to the Long Engine Shed in Piston Road and ask for Luke the custodian. The railway connection may surprise you at first but it is of the very essence since there would have been no Rug but for the men of the six lines that once converged here.

But first let's see how things began. Imagine a gaunt and smoky lamp-lit room round about 1840 filled with twenty or so off-shift railwaymen. It is all the mean owners in their posh London clubs will provide for the recreation of these worthy men. The air is cold and damp and boots are weighed down by a footplate slurry of coal dust and ash. But all is not in gloom for these bold men of rail have hearty souls and among them is Tich Evans, a man of courage and song who will lead them on.

And so it was that one Friday in December of extreme frost and cold, the steam from engine funnels freezing as snowflakes, the boots of the men froze to the floor of their sorrowful rest room so that none could move, not even an inch.

But to the rescue came the song of Tich Evans whose *Cwm Rhondda* notes warmed the cockled toes of all present to precipitate an instant and crackling thaw. Not only that but he carried a copy of The Illustrated London News left that day in a first class carriage which contained prints of wealthy plutocrats warming their doeskin feet in deep-piled luxury rugs.

"Brothers of the footplate," spoke Evans. "Let us show these rich exploiters of the proletariat that we are no less able than they to protect the comfort of our unpampered feet and honest boots. Let each of us combine in solidarity with all to make our own great rug; each comrade with his sisters to make one square foot a month at a cost of sixpence, and if this means forgoing ale, so be it."

There was an immediate shout of approval and the work began at once.

Very soon squares of rug began to appear in the long engine shed for assembly where the joy of workers' success spread into song:

Cold boots have gone
Cold boots have gone
So join us in our workers song
Though some may scoff and others jeer
We'll keep the great Rug growing here

So today when you view this great work in silent and respectful meditation, just recall the bravery of these noble men and show them honour. Sit a while on an old railway bench and let it all soak in.

Keith Marshall

June 21: Thankless Servitude

It is the same every day. The sun rises outside, I can see it through a gap in the curtains. I sometimes wonder what it is like outside, but I'm never taken out. With the morning comes the clatter of footfalls from upstairs and my gut clenches with dread anticipation. I always hope it will be different but the thunder of fast approaching feet coming down the stairs signals that today will be no different.

Even though I know it is coming, the sudden opening of the door makes me jump and nervous butterflies spin in my stomach. It's not long before the long-legged teen sits on the right side of my chest throwing all his weight down upon me; it hurts and I struggle to breathe. I can hear his laughter cruelly ringing in my ears. His back obscures the vision in my right eye.

Then the smaller fatter one sits on my left side and although I let out a cry of anguish and suffering, these two tormentors ignore it and continue to sit atop me as if I were nothing more than a mere object to be used at their whim. I can still see through my left eye and the television is turned on, where I see others of my kind being cruelly treated and sold into slavery.

Try as I might my arms are too far apart to be effectual in freeing myself from the crushing weight of these two monsters. The long-legged one shifts and pins my right arm down, scratching it with some kind of utensil. Then the big bad comes in with two steaming hot bowls of some indescribable mush and the two terrors on me wriggle and adjust themselves without a care in the world for me or my feelings.

I feel a shudder run through me as they begin to greedily consume the mush. A drop of it falls from the small fat one's utensil and the scalding hot stuff hits my flesh, and although I scream in agony not one of them lifts a finger to help me. What did I do to deserve this fate?

That's when the female arrives. She yells at the small fat one, "What have you spilt on the couch?" There's no real concern for my welfare however; after all these years of thankless servitude, they still have not bothered to learn my name.

Christopher Trezise

June 22: Slave Girl

Eilif strutted along the edge of the meadow, careful not to crush the long grass. It was close to midsummer and in a few days the village would be out to cut the hay. He glanced up at the sky. Clear blue, without a cloud visible, good for a few days yet.

He had told his wife he was going fishing. That was not entirely true. She had been nagging him to repair the fence around their house, but it was too hot to start splitting wood. Much better to spend the time beside the river, especially on the day that the women did the washing. It was not a popular job most of the year, but on this blazing hot day, it was the best place to be.

He had his eye on a new girl, a slave recently arrived in the village with hair like silken gold. He had exchanged glances with her in the hall one evening and she appeared willing. At least he should be able to get a better look at her body, everyone got soaked on wash day, and in this heat, many would remove their outer clothing.

Sweat ran down his back and he slowed his pace. The sound of splashing water almost drowned the buzz of insects on the last flowers scattered amongst the grasses. He moved faster, then stopped as a figure stepped out in front of him, a hooded stranger. One of the expected wedding guests? He must be stifling under the thick wool.

Eilif heard a loud splash and laughter. It sounded like the new slave.

"Excuse me, I'm in a hurry." As he pushed past the stranger, strong fingers grabbed his hair and jerked back his head. A cool whisper touched his throat, followed by a flood of heat. He stared upwards. Silhouetted against the dark blue was a sickle, blood dripping from the freshly sharpened edge. His blood?

The sky darkened and the stranger lowered him carefully to the ground.

Christine Hancock

June 23: On The Farm

I remember when my career working on farms began. I was half way through my O-level course when mother found out that I had to work on a farm for a year before I could apply to an agricultural college, especially as I lived in a suburb of Birmingham.

She found me a place as a farm pupil in Bradworthy in Devon. As dad did not drive and we did not own a car then, our good neighbour Harold hired us a Standard Vanguard, big enough for us all, and drove us all the way. It was down a mile-long track off the road. I thought it a lovely place and as soon as I had been introduced, off all my family went, leaving me there. I was 15. I was given 15 shillings a week and spent most of it on sweets to compensate for the homesickness. No wonder I am still overweight!

If you have ever been left to pick up boulders in a field and load them into a trailer all day on your own; or if you have wheeled a wheelbarrow to shovel up the fresh cowpats dropped there by the cows earlier that morning; milked the cows twice a day and bedded them down with straw in the shippon cowshed and still love the job, well you have picked you correct career.

I had the job of exercising the brood mare called Kate. She was 15 hands high and in foal and broad too. I am 5ft only; they would hitch me up onto her back. I couldn't reach to put my feet in the stirrups so just had them in the leathers.

And off we would go. The farm track had little streams running over it. At the first one, she would put her head down for a drink and I would slide off into the stream. Kate would wait patiently for me and then I would walk her for the rest of our walk. I had to do my own washing, a thing I'd never done before, and Mrs Jarvis liked to check my drawers for tidiness too.

I am still not tidy but I survived it all.

Ruth Hughes

June 24: A Room With A View

The radio station had spoken of nothing else for weeks. Tens of thousands of people were expected so I visited the street two days earlier to identify the best viewpoint. Just like everyone else, I had to be in the right place. Watching from street level would only work if I could guarantee being at the front of the crowd so I had found a nice spot on a slightly raised grassed area just by a tree which would provide shade from the morning sun and help me clearly see the main event.

The early morning was warming up and already very sunny. The crowds had gathered since dawn to ensure a good position to witness the grand procession. The street vendors were out in force supplying refreshments and the usual paraphernalia of flags, banners and photographs.

I arrived early but it was already busier than the radio station had predicted. Worse still 'my' spot had been taken by a large and very noisy family. I knew straight away that they were there for the duration.

I began to panic as the morning rolled on. I was going to miss everything. I could feel the sweat starting to spread across my whole body. Carrying my picnic bag didn't help either as the sun intensified.

Looking around I suddenly saw how I just might be able to save the day. I ran along the street weaving between the growing and increasingly solid rows of anticipating watchers. Occasionally bumping into someone and shouting "sorry, sorry", I never stopped. There was no time to waste.

Soon I was at the entrance to the building and ran up flights of stairs sometimes stumbling and using the handrail to support my flagging momentum. Finally, enough was enough. It had to be this floor, I couldn't go on. But as it turned out the view from the window was just right. I rummaged through my 'picnic bag' and within minutes the cavalcade turned into view. This was it. As I took aim, I muttered, "Goodbye Mr President."

William Philpott

June 25: In The Blood

With a smile on my face, I head down Upper Street to the small café where Suzanne has asked me to meet her. In my book I imagined David's research facility to be in the opposite direction. A huge building about ten minutes' walk the other way. It's fun to have my fiction brought to life like this.

I soon find the café. I take a deep breath, flick my mind back to the picture I saw of Suzanne Royall on her website, and I make my way inside.

I immediately see her sitting towards the back on a rather large table. She's a glamorous lady wearing a stunning black suit. She has long, thick cherry hair and a beautiful face, and I can't help but find her instantly intimidating.

I take another deep breath. She's here to help me. I give myself a moment to feel proud, telling myself what an amazing moment this is. Then I head on over.

"Suzanne?" I ask.

"Penelope Fox?" I normally love it when people say my actual name, it's so much nicer than stupid Loppy. But on this occasion there is a bitterness in her tone. That's something I wasn't expecting.

"Nice to meet you," I say extending my hand out, but all I get in return is an icy glare.

I take my coat and scarf off and place them neatly on the back of the chair.

A waiter appears at our side. "Are you ready to order?" the young man asks.

"Not yet," Suzanne remarks. "We're waiting for one other person to join us."

"Who's joining us?" I nervously ask, guessing that it must be her business partner or assistant.

"Like you don't know," she responds, quite to the point.

My pride has now totally been replaced with a deeply uncomfortable sensation. I get the feeling this woman hates me. What have I done? My book wasn't that bad. I really don't know what to say.

"What is it you want?" a male voice suddenly says from behind me and it makes the hairs on my neck stand on end. I shiver as the voice is unnervingly familiar.

The man sits down next to Suzanne. I look across at him and instantly my jaw drops open.

In every single possible way it's the man that I imagined. He's like a real life David Royall. The way he styles his dark brown hair without any particular effort, his crystal blue eyes that are so light yet also have so much depth, his firm mannerisms and serious face that hide how soft he really is inside: it's the man I know so well. It's the man I've been dreaming about and it's the man that I've just written twenty-eight chapters about.

I suddenly realise that he's staring at me with equal levels of surprise.

"I think I have a right to know what's going on here," Suzanne demands.

I want to reply but I just don't have any words.

"Why have you written a story about my husband?" she spits at me. She now has venom in her eyes.

Royall! It suddenly clicks with me that she's Suzanne Royall. "Is your name David Royall?" I utter. I find myself glaring in awe at the totally real man opposite me. He doesn't reply, though. He just glares at me in return. There are no words to sum up what the hell is going on.

Suzanne turns her fierce eyes away from me and her next question is aimed very much at David. "Are you having an affair?"

"Don't be ridiculous," he snaps. "I work fifteen hour days and then I come home to you. When do you suppose I have time for an affair?"

"Then why has this pathetic girl written about you? She knows everything about you. Every little detail. Where you work, how you like your coffee, which side of the bed you have to sleep on. How could she know that if you hadn't slept with her?"

This is too much for me. I can feel my heart starting to patter. I have to get out of here. I really don't feel well at all.

"I don't know what's going on, but there's clearly been some sort of mistake," I say with a shaky voice. "I'm sorry for any trouble I've caused you. It's just a coincidence. I've never seen this man before in my life and I promise neither of you will ever see me again."

With that I scramble to get my coat and scarf and I rush out of the café as quickly as I can. I pace back to the tube.

I step in the station and immediately flop against the wall to catch my breath. That was probably the most awkward, embarrassing and awful experience of my entire life. What was it all about?

I suddenly feel a hand on my shoulder. "Are you okay?" a warm voice asks.

I look up and see the glistening eyes of David. I step away from him, worried what he's going to do next.

"I'm sorry about that," he says. "My wife can be a little over-dramatic at times."

We spend a few moments just staring at each other, breathing each other in. How could he be real?

"How do you know me?" he finally says. Before I get a chance to reply though, he adds, "And how do I know you?"

Lindsay Woodward

June 26: Jack's House

In case you're wondering, it is a long way to Tipperary. Especially when you catch the night train from Holyhead and endure a rough crossing. Dublin was exciting; I longed to stay and explore but the train was leaving for Nenagh, clanking and steaming impatiently, so I climbed aboard – final destination Borrisokane, a village to the north of Nenagh.

The address I'd been given was simply 'Jacks' house'.

"Everyone knows Jack," they said, "you'll have no trouble." But there were no house names, or numbers. I asked a local for directions: "Now which Jack would that be?" he asked, not surprisingly.

However, the cottage, when I finally found it, was very pretty. I was relieved to find the key fitted the lock, confirming that this was the right house! Inside it was cosy and quaint: dried peat stacked by the fireplace, rugs on the floor, food in the pantry – but no bath, no shower, and no hot water either!

I went shopping; there were eighteen shops, all general stores, and all sold everything from bread, fresh meat and groceries to coal, wood, creosote, horse fodder and newspapers, dog food, fly swatters, hand knitted jumpers, and sweets. Adorning the till and the shelves were holy pictures of Jesus and the Virgin Mary, rosaries and crucifixes dangled, but there was genuine kindness, and welcome advice.

There was usually a story or two told by the shopkeeper too, so it was just as well no-one was in a hurry. Like the man who paid a thousand pounds for a racing greyhound with which to make his fortune, put the dog in the boot of his car, only to lose it the moment he got home. He opened the boot! The greyhound shot out, and bolted down the road, never to be seen again. Neither the dog nor his money!

The landscape was emerald green and very beautiful. On country walks I was surprised to see the occasional Christian grotto by the roadside, decorated with flowers and candles. I also came across houses in various stages of being built but mysteriously abandoned. I was told all builders had second jobs as funeral directors, and didn't have much spare time, or money, to finish them. But the whole place seemed to have an innocence about it, and no pressure to finish anything. It was as if everyone had all the time in the world; they would stop and chat without any reserve.

But on Sunday morning the whole of Borrisokane came to a standstill. Dozens of cars were parked, or more accurately just abandoned outside the Catholic church, some blocking the road as everyone attended mass. And it's true what they say; when Mass finished, everyone spilled out and went straight into the pub!

Theresa Le Flem

June 27: Grandma's House

Grandma's house was a small, busy and happy place. The furniture was large with lots of colourful cushions. High wooden chairs sat around a very high table. I remember climbing up the chair like a ladder and Grandma putting two cushions under my bottom so that I could reach the table. All life happened in that room. There was always a fire crackling in the hearth and the smell of something cooking in the air. Grandma sat in her rocking chair laughing, all jolly and cuddly. She never got really cross. When we were little and a little bit cheeky, she would say, "I'll slap your bottom with a wet lettuce leaf." We would shriek and laugh. We laughed a lot at grandma's house.

Pulling up outside the house, I was immediately struck by how small it appeared, and how run down it had become. The window frames were splitting and the paint was peeling off in leaf shapes, like a flower shedding its petals. The wooden front door was warped and I had to push hard with my shoulder to open it.

Inside, the living room was the same. The sofa with the colourful cushions, the wooden table and chairs still tucked in the corner. Grandma's big rocking chair still stood by the fire and Grandma was sitting on it, or rather in it. She had shrunk to a tiny fragile porcelain doll like figure. She was surrounded by her embroidered cushions, with a colourful crocheted rug over her legs. Her feet didn't touch the floor. I wondered how many cushions she would need under her bottom to reach the table?

It seemed as though Grandma's furniture had grown as she got older, and I had become a giant! The fire still glowed and the comforting smells still lingered, but the laughter and happiness had diminished with Grandma's stature. Her laugh was now a light tinkling sound, like a fairy bell. I was afraid to do more than smile for fear of breaking something.

Linda Slate

June 28: Lucky Break?

At first, I thought the letter had to be a scam. What do they say? If it seems too good to be true, it probably is. I do not purchase National Lottery tickets. Getting gullible people to gamble is a deceitful way of raising money. And... the odds of actually winning anything are so pitifully low, a ticket is simply not worth wasting your money on; so I don't!

My son bought me a ticket though, for my birthday. It was a joke really, to heckle as I preached from my soap-box, to topple me from my hobby horse.

He texted me the other day, "Hey Dad, looks like your number's come up, what you going to do now?" I didn't bother to check anything, anywhere. I wouldn't know where to even start. But now, thud, right on my doormat. What will I do with 1.2 million quid? Can't just stick it in my bank account, can I?

Blimey though, the holidays we could have, Maureen'd love it. The car I could drive. The house we could get. Crikey we could employ a cleaner! Presents, gifts galore for the whole family. The grandchildren, my old workmates, our neighbours. Everyone...every damn person I know!

Everyone? All the family? The entire neighbourhood, that we would be moving away from? How many of us worked at the factory for a start? And where would I stop? How much should I give? Do you pay tax if you win a load of money? I'd have to hire an accountant!

Publicity! You get known, don't you? You get pestered by 'good causes'. Begging letters? Threats even! I'd have to go into hiding.

+   +

My phone buzzes. I stare at the screen, but I can't answer. Son, what have you done? What have you done?

Steve Redshaw

June 29: Great-Auntie Gertie

Once a year, Great-Auntie Gertie, my grandad's sister, took a bus and visited us. Straight out of a Victorian photograph, Great-Auntie Gertie was the epitome of a little old lady, complete with button-up shoes, dark brown dress planted with tiny flowers, a lace modesty vest pinned at the neck, and spectacles with lenses so thick that you could not see her eyes.

My mam said Great-Auntie Gertie had strained them while hand-decorating china tea-services, an occupational hazard, except my mam did not use that term.

Once a year, we, my mam and me, visited Great-Auntie Gertie. All I remember of her house is the room we sat in, dark as if in permanent dusk, net-curtained, filled to overflowing. Once seated in a chair, it was impossible to move. A great organ glowered along one wall; a grandfather clock peered down, missing the occasional heart beat. The mantelpiece of a huge black-leaded grate jostled with oddments and ornaments guarded by a pair of Staffordshire china dogs.

"Those are for you, Doris, when I die."

Every surface was shrouded with lace or embroidered covers to keep off the dust, not very successfully. A giant-sized table groaned under piles of papers, pots and pans, tea-drugged cups, half-finished knitting, an enormous vase with flowers that had long since lost the will to live, and brown paper-bagged pieces of ham sandwiches, in the vernacular, and Chorley cakes that my mam had brought for our tea.

Then the great moment. "Would you like a drop of my home-made parsnip wine, Doris?"

"Go on then, just a drop."

So Great Auntie Gertie would bend her creaking back and search at the back of her sideboard, to bring out a bottle with a flourish. My eyes were glued as she poured the pale yellow liquor into two cups.

"Would you like a little drop, duckie?"

So another little cup was brought out for me to sup. I love parsnips.

But one year, horror of horrors, at the bottom of the cup lay a huge black cockroach. We all stared at it. That was the last time we sampled

Great-Auntie Gertie's home-made wine. It was also the last time we visited Great-Auntie Gertie. She died soon afterwards.

We never did get her Staffordshire china dogs.

Wendy Goulstone

June 30: Gnomes

Her name was Anna Pascoe, 55 years old. She had lived in the same middle terrace house that she had been born in. She was a seamstress by profession, mending and turning hems and also making anything anyone required including wedding dresses. She made a comfortable living.

Anna's hobby was collecting gnomes. She kept them all in her little front garden in serried ranks; she knew every one personally.

Her very favourite one was called Jeremy. He was a little bigger than the rest and holding a fishing rod though he never caught anything. He had a red hat, blue waistcoat, blue trousers and green wellies in case he had to wade in. He had rosy cheeks and a slightly bulbous nose. People travelling along the road on the hourly bus would smile when passing the house and children loved to see her collection.

Then, one day, Jeremy disappeared. Anna notified the police but they couldn't drum up much enthusiasm for one gnome. They pointed out she had plenty more to be going on with!

Then the postcards started to arrive - from Germany, France, Italy, Belgium and many other parts of the world.

Anna put them in an album. They all had a photo of Jeremy on them and said how much he was enjoying his holiday.

Anna did not know what to do. She thought if she notified the papers, people would only laugh at her, and she couldn't bear that.

Then, one day, exactly nine months later, Jeremy reappeared back in pride of place looking none the worse from his adventures - maybe a little smug and pleased with himself - and, on the end of his fishing rod, a beautiful rainbow trout.

Ruth Hughes

A Story for Every Day of Summer

July

July 1: We Shall Prevail

The courtroom was panelled in dark wood, lit by hundreds of candles in chandeliers, in wall sconces, in candelabra on the lawyers' desks and the judge's bench. There were no windows. The jurors had to make do with rushlights. They flinched away from the heat and the flames, sweat pouring down their faces. None of them wanted to be there, but they had no choice. And no choice in the verdict.

Guards surrounded the prisoners, who were weighed down with chains and iron shackles. Their leader stared arrogantly at the judge, splendid in his wig and crimson robes.

"How do you plead?" the clerk asked. The men stayed mute.

The judge stood and led the lawyers, crow-like in their black gowns, and the jurors from the courtroom to the arena where the people of the town waited in silence. The guards followed with the prisoners.

The instruments of justice had been prepared: the cauldron of boiling water suspended over a blazing fire, the path of red-hot ploughshares, the iron bar plunged into a brazier. The masked inquisitor waited patiently, arms folded, ready to perform his appointed tasks.

"You stand accused of high treason against the lawful king of this land," the judge said. He dropped a gold ring into the steaming cauldron. "If you can take this ring or walk this path or carry the iron bar for three paces, without injury to your body, your innocence is proved. If not, then you stand condemned. Let the trial begin."

The leader of the rebels stepped forward. He turned to his men and said, "We have protected the weak and the poor against the powers of tyranny." He pointed at the cauldron, the red-hot path and the red-hot iron bar. "These things are sent to try us, but we shall prevail."

Fran Neatherway

July 2: The Walk

The sun burned down fiercely onto a dry, barren landscape, as far as the eye could see. At the top of the ridge Si took a sip from his water bottle, and with one last look behind him, at the green oasis, set off across the unimaginably huge crater, aiming for the narrow gap on the far side. It was going to take days, and everything he needed was on the sledge he pulled behind him. Almost everything. He'd expected to find more water than he actually had, and he'd expected it to be drinkable. It wasn't.

Gauging distances in a featureless world is very deceptive, and by the time the sun approached the horizon Si could see no difference in the distance to the gap, and despite walking continuously for six hours, the ridge behind seemed no further away. He didn't dare stop moving as there was no guessing what might appear once the darkness fell.

"Only mad dogs and Englishmen," Si said quietly. He kept moving throughout that night and the next day, and by then the far edge of the crater seemed a little closer. The Wide-Awake pills seemed to be working well, but he was having to severely ration his meagre water supply. Si hoped the equipment he was going to collect was worth all the effort.

As the sun rose on the sixth morning, the gap in the crater rim was within reach, and through it the glint of sun on metal shone blindingly. At noon Si walked in through the mother-ship's door, and was handed a large packet by Roger, with the words, "Tell Stevie-boy not to blow these up!"

After filling the water tanks in the sledge, and picking up a new box of Wide-Awake pills, Si inspected the package and put it safely into the pannier. As he put on his helmet and tested the oxygen supply, he grinned at Roger, gave him a thumbs up, then toggled his microphone ON, and said...

"This is the last time I offer to go for chips."

EE Blythe

July 3: Changing Destinations

I have found that whenever you plan something very carefully, it never works out. Like the time we were transferred from Ocean Island to Christmas Island. We were informed that we would be sailing in 'about a month'.

Arrangements were made for crates and especially farewell meals. There was also the added treat that the Bishop of Tarawa was going to visit and, as we wouldn't have a priest on Christmas Island, the Bishop was going to give Susan her First Communion. Everything was planned down to the last detail. The men who had worked for John were going to pack the main crates, and a friend was going to make the dress during the next two weeks.

The next day was, to put it mildly, panic stations on all fronts. A ship had arrived with instructions to take us on board together with our crates (containing all our possessions) to sail within 24 hours. I had done some packing but this was a bit much. I had been with my friend, just about to cut the material for Sue's dress. I don't think I had ever worked so fast. Cancellation of meals. Apologies to the Bishop and his staff and packing our belongings. Yes. We did it with the kind help of the Gilbert team, and help from our friends.

We sailed from Ocean Island to Melbourne to connect with another ship to Christmas Island. While waiting for the final ship, Susan was given the 'treat' of receiving her First Communion.

This wasn't the first time I had had a change of destination. Five years earlier, I had boarded a ship for Australia, north of Sidney, and then found within a couple of hours of sailing that we had been directed to Christchurch in New Zealand. That time we thought that the officers on the ship had been joking. Not until I received a telegram from John telling me to make sure that the company paid for my flight to Australia, did we believe the officers.

Pam Barton

July 4: Rocco

Rocco scanned the job advertisements, a humbling experience in itself. He had been in the family business for 35 years and knew nothing else. He was a professional clown

At parties he often joked: "If the car passed its MOT, I'd get a new garage." Retirement loomed and Rocco dreaded not hearing laughter, not smelling the popcorn or not hearing Clive's announcement: "Panaro Brothers present Rocco the side-splitting Clown-prince of Comedy."

A fake bucket of water, fast pratfalls and extending clown shoes were all it took to get the crowd roaring, at least in the 80s. More evil clowns, more TV jokers, more anxiety generally and the slow decline of the clown's prestige meant the Panaros were letting him go.

The job centre was small, as suits a rural town in Shropshire near Rocco's home. It had been his mother's decades ago. She wanted him to be an accountant but even in sixth form he enjoyed making people laugh. Like the time he drank a bottle of Quink or came into school wearing a dog collar... with the lead still attached.

"Mr Richards. The advisor can see you now."

The nondescript pot-bellied gent in his mid-fifties walked over, separated by the glass anti-Covid panel.

"How symbolic," he thought as the advisor, Miss Grey, spoke.

"Not enough NI contributions, Mr Richards, so no benefit entitlement." Panaro had penny-pinched everywhere to the point of criminality. No point complaining.

"Also, Mr Richards, could you please attend your interview in your work attire next fortnight?"

It was true. Rhys (his real name) was wearing clothes more suitable for his allotment than his benefit sign-on interview but it gave him a great idea.

A little boy pulled on his sleeve. "Rocco! I saw you when I was on holiday. I giggled when you and Dromio got so messy!" His mother pulled him away.

Two weeks later. Same sign on day, same harassed mother and

cheerful little son as Rhys a.k.a Rocco joined the queue, wearing a strange black Macintosh. There were several young men in the centre for construction CSCS card training and two police officers along with the usual security and staff.

One of the more sharp-eyed security officers witnessed the transformation: coat off, white makeup on face, blue star on left side, yellow hat on head, reversible coat bright red and weirdly extending shoes now the size of divers flippers.

Rhys Richards was gone. Rocco stood in his place. At this stage, a number of clients noticed Rocco and the queue dispersed like billiard balls on a break. Only the lady, with the cheerful little son, was engrossed with her phone and missed the commotion.

"Mummy! Look! It's the funny clown!"

She was startled and waved Rocco past coulrophobically.

"Is Miss Grey available yet? I'm a little early."

The co-ordinator said nothing and waved him through 15 minutes early. Rocco sat down in front of the amazed advisor. Rocco offered her a Top Deck pack still with the cards inside.

"Miss Grey, pick a card." Unwisely she pulled out a two of spades which made a noise like a Christmas cracker. The construction trainees were already chuckling.

Miss Grey got the first flyer leaflet.

Then Rocco handed more leaflets to the construction students; eventually most of the clients and staff had a leaflet.

"My new business adventure," said Rocco to the weary police officers. He left the job centre with a somersault and no leaflets, and walked down the street producing free balloons for any children whose parents would allow it.

Back at the centre, Miss Grey read the leaflet out loud. It said, '*Join Rocco's School for Clowns*' above a pair of crossed slapsticks and the face of an auguste.

"Funny! R.S.C," said security.

Everyone fell about laughing.

Chris Wright

July 5: Missing

The lights of the last bus disappeared round the corner. She stood staring at the space where it had been, cursing the driver, annoyed with herself for not getting there on time, angry with him for refusing to drive her home after their break-up, for not offering to walk with her to the bus stop. She was smouldering with rage, about the deceit, the lies, that woman. And she was afraid, too, of his counter accusations, his threats; the way his fists were clenched so that the knuckles were white; the way his eyes pierced her.

And now she had missed the last bus. There was nothing for it but to turn back down the hill towards the house, the bag hanging heavily from her shoulder. How would he react when she rang the door-bell?

A few cars passed, but no-one else was about. They were all in bed by ten here, in houses tucked away down long, tree-lined drives.

At the intersection with the motorway, the mouth of the underpass gaped. Of course, there was nothing to fear. Fifteen minutes ago, she had walked through and seen no-one. There was no choice, whatever the consequences. She had to go on, to the house, where he would be.

At the bottom of the ramp she turned right into the tunnel, triggering the dim lights. She quickened her step, feeling trapped, anxious to be out in the open again. Half way. Not far to go, now.

Then she was in darkness. Pitch black. She stopped, heart thumping, uncertain what to do. She stretched out her arms and made her way to the wall of the tunnel, feeling her way along it, one thought hammering her brain. Her hand touched coarse wool. Warm breath settled on her face.

Wendy Goulstone

July 6: The Sneezy Princess

An Un-Romantic Fairy-Tale - Not for children or people of a nervous disposition.

Once upon a time there was a fairy princess. And she lived in a big, beautiful fairy castle. And her name was... well, don't look at me, I don't know. And do you know? Every morning she sneezed six times!

For a few moments after she awoke, she would seem as normal as you or me. But then Achoo! Aachoo! Aaachoo! Aaaachoo! Aaaaachoo! AAAAAACHOO!!!

For the fairies in the castle, who never had to get up to do any work, this was a real pain. They would be sound asleep at half past eleven in the morning, with at least another three hours of solid snoozing to do when suddenly they'd be jerked awake by the first sneeze.

They'd just be dropping back to sleep when the second sneeze came.

Thinking that two sneezes had gone and that would be it, they'd turn over and start to snooze again, but then the third sneeze would sledgehammer them. After five sneezes, they'd be really annoyed.

By this time, they knew it wouldn't be any good resting their head back on the pillow because - wait for it - I said, "Wait for it!"- ROAR! There goes the sixth sneeze. Everyone in the castle would be wide awake by now and there would be no choice but to get up and go for their daily dip in the fairy pond.

Well, as you can imagine, all the fairies in the beautiful fairy castle tried their favourite remedies. The fairy princess took powders and potions, smeared loathsome ointments on her nose, she stood on one leg under a full moon on a third Tuesday at midnight holding a rose in her teeth and with a corn plaster on her right ear. (Didn't you know that one? Works every time. Well, almost every time. Well, actually, as you ask, not this time in particular.)

No, nothing worked. So they called in all the fairy magicians who... well, you can guess what they tried. But that didn't work, not even a bit.

So they shot her. **Phillip Gregge**

July 7: Almost Broken

"Do you still love me?" Lee asked, flopping down on the worn settee, almost spilling his can of lager.

"Of course I do," Sophie replied from an armchair across the room. It too was threadbare, as was pretty much the whole house.

"You're just being a bit weird," Lee said.

"I'm not."

"Eight cans cost less than a tenner. We can afford a tenner."

"I know."

"You can have a beer too if you want," Lee offered.

"No thanks."

"Are you going to be like this all night?"

"I'm just waiting for my soap to come on."

"If that's more important than me."

Sophie focused intently on the television.

"I saw that Nathan today," Lee said, immediately grabbing Sophie's attention.

"My ex Nathan?" she asked.

"Just after I'd come out of the pub at lunchtime. I had to say something."

"Like what?"

"I wanted to let him know what he'd lost. Remind him that you're mine now."

"Hasn't he got a new girlfriend?"

"Come on. It's obvious he still fancies you."

"Even if he does, what does it matter? I'm with you now."

"Do you still love him?"

"Of course not."

"Then why did your head flick up so urgently when I mentioned his name?"

"I was surprised to hear you talk about him."

"Surprised or excited?"

"Leave it out. My soap's starting now."

"What if he wanted to get back together?" Lee pushed.

"I'm with you now," Sophie replied.

"What if you weren't with me?"

"Please can we drop this."

"I was just-"

"Please," Sophie begged, cutting him off.

Lee shrugged as he took another gulp of his beer, but nerves started crawling through Sophie. Was Lee just winding her up, or was this going to erupt into something she couldn't control?

"What did Nathan say?" she asked.

There was a tense silence before Lee said, "Nothing."

"What did Nathan say, Lee?" Sophie repeated, her heart pounding.

"Nothing. We had a laugh. He's a nice bloke, okay. It made me wonder why you're with me when you could be with him. Then I remembered that he dumped you."

"It's all in the past."

Lee snapped to his feet in anger. "Just admit it," he shouted. "You still love him, don't you?

"No! Absolutely not."

"Don't give me that. I saw your eyes when I mentioned his name."

"Surprise?"

"Lust."

"What?"

Lee stomped across the room and stood above Sophie menacingly.

"Admit you still love him."

"I don't."

"Admit it."

"I won't admit something that's not true."

"Admit it!"

Lee slapped Sophie hard across the face.

She took the blow. If she took it quietly, he usually skulked away. Silence was her only power.

"I won't admit something that's not true," she finally muttered. "Can I get back to my programme now?"

Lee didn't move for a few moments. Then he turned and flopped back down on the settee.

"I only get jealous because I love you so much," he mumbled.

"I know," Sophie said. Although truthfully she no longer knew anything for sure.

"Do you still love me?" he asked.

Sophie stared at the telly in silence.

Lindsay Woodward

July 8: The Story Of A Car

Ken (aged 5): Brmm brmm. When I grow up, I want a car like this that I can drive in and I will take you anywhere you want to go.

Granny: You'll have to get a good job, Ken. That's a Ferrari.

Ken (aged 15): My family is so poor. I'm... I'm so fed up... so fed up, Mark. I don't ever want to have to work in a warehouse.

Mark: At least it's honest work.

Ken (aged 25): My business is going from bad to worse, might be time to change to selling insurance. That's what is going to be big, financial services. Mark, what will writing get you?

Ken (aged 35): BigJuice (tm) has done so well, now I can get that motor I've always dreamed of and I'm off on holiday in the USA.

Mark: If you take your eyes off your spreadsheets for five minutes, you might get to meet the woman of your dreams.

Ken (aged 55): I can't believe she's gone.

Mark: Nice service, Ken, went really well. Did Denise ask for the Ferrari in the cortege? I thought she hated it.

Ken: She did and called it the 'other woman'.

Mark: Just you and 'her' now then.

Ken: I'm selling it.

Chris Wright

July 9: A Sachet Of Sauce

Once upon a time, there was a woman called Ruth and her neighbour Sylvia. They lived in a village, on the main road opposite a thatched pub and popular restaurant. This was in 1970.

On Saturday nights, Ruth's husband took care of their children, while she and Sylvia became waitresses for the evening. They served all the people who booked to dine.

The landlord's son was a great chef. Then they cleared and washed up and re-laid the tables. When all was done, the two of them sat down for their own steak supper served with a jug of tartare sauce to pour onto their steaks. It was such a treat especially as Ruth's family were not well off and certainly could not afford steak.

They enjoyed their supper chatting together, cleared up and, clutching their wages, went happily home. It was not just the supper or just the wages and company, but for Ruth it was the chance to feel like a person in her own right - not just a housewife and a mother. It was a sachet of tartare sauce in a cafe that stirred up this memory.

Ruth Hughes

July 10: Storm

The wind whipped across the puddles, sending the spray horizontally along the promenade, drenching their legs. They sought sanctuary in a cafe, took off their wet coats and sat by the window, hands clasped round mugs of hot soup, watching the waves crashing against the cliffs. The plate glass stifled the roar and splash as they sat in silence.

At last, they relinquished their seats, hovered by the door, hoping for a lull, and then dashed out into the rain. The wind was forced through the narrow funnel between the church and the row of closed shops, spinning them round as they tried to control umbrellas.

The footpath round the promontory would have been suicidal. Instead, they walked on to the sheltered harbour, where, at last, the wind abated, though waves pounded against the harbour wall, pouring over the top.

Next morning, the sun broke through the cloud. The ghost of a rainbow hung over the town.

In their hotel room, the storm still raged.

Wendy Goulstone

July 11: Itchy Trousers

It was the day after the school trip to the Black Country Museum. I was 10 and bubbling with excitement as we'd just been given a writing task. The best sort of lesson. We'd been told to write about our experience at the museum.

I carefully considered my options. I didn't want to just write the same things as everyone else. I thought about the transport we'd seen, the sweet shop, the manufacturing, but it all seemed too obvious. Then I remembered how we'd been told what life was like for a ten-year-old in the nineteenth century. The man had said that the boys had to wear really itchy trousers. It had stayed with me, as if of all the things we'd learnt that day, itchy trousers were the most unpleasant feature of nineteenth century life. I felt so passionate about this torment, I instantly put pen to paper.

The next day, when our work had been marked, I received a house point from my teacher. That was the most significant symbol of good work that a ten-year-old could get. Although she was giggling as she handed it to me. The following day my work was put up on the wall and other teachers were invited to read about the struggle of itchy trousers. They all laughed, as if they had no care at all for the suffering of those poor boys. My peers weren't laughing. Why were the adults?

I wondered if one day I'd understand what was so funny. I re-read my work, but I couldn't find anything amusing about it. Oh well, at least I didn't have to wear itchy trousers. I was grateful for that.

Lindsay Woodward

July 12: Sandwood Bay

"You must go to Sandwood Bay. It's a four mile walk but it is the best beach in Scotland." So we went. A derelict cottage marked the deserted bay. The tide was going out as we strode along the shore, looking for treasure.

In a little pool of water lay a sea-smooth pebble. A streak of white quartz glinted against black basalt. A cloud covered the sun and the wind sharpened. I put the stone in my pocket and fastened my fleece.

"Let's go," I said. It was almost dark when we reached the cottage.

"Put it back."

"What did you say?"

"I didn't say anything," he said.

"Put it back."

A strange fear gripped me. I put my hands in my pockets and my fingers wrapped round the pebble.

"Put it back."

"I don't like this stone," I said. "I don't want it."

"Throw it away then."

"I have to put it back."

"Don't be ridiculous. It looks like we're in for a storm. We'll get soaked."

"I have to go back. I have to put it where it belongs."

He saw the terror in my eyes. Together we ran back to the little pool.

"Put it back." We watched the wet sand suck the stone down, turned and ran until our chests ached.

Back at the village, we heard stories of a storm at sea, of a shipwreck, a drowned boy, a bearded sailor, of footsteps heard by campers at night but no sign of footprints in the sand in the morning, and of accidents that befell those who took objects from the beach.

Wendy Goulstone

July 13: Imagination

I heard the seagull call, and looked up into the overbright sun, just in time to see the gull wheel away. The sun was blinding, and my eyes screwed up to a tight slit. I heard another gull cry, and another, closer this time, but I couldn't see them through the prismatic rainbow distortion of my almost closed eyes.

I stood, eyes shut, with my hands on the rail, and lifted my head again, this time to feel the sun beating down on my face. And on my shoulders, warming me to my bones. I slowed my breathing and let my senses fly free to taste the day.

The air was rich with the scent of summer flowers, rose, honeysuckle, orange blossom, touched now and again with odd wafts of vanilla, and less welcome, fried onion.

Far off there was a dog yapping excitedly, and a child's voice. Maybe the child was throwing a stick, or more safely, a ball for the dog, or maybe throwing the ball to another child, a friend or sibling. Too far off for words to be discernable.

Closer were the noises of the occasional car, and now and again, the odd bicycle wheel whirred past me. Presumably with the rest of the cycle attached to it. But no-one spoke, or called a cheery 'Hello!'

A warm, soft breeze touched my cheek, gently, intermittently, and teasingly lifted my hair, streaming it across my nose and mouth. Something papery flapped into my ankle, and was gone.

A letterbox clattered, post or newspaper I idly wondered. And all the time the almost regular susurration of the waves was lulling me to sleep.

Only, it wasn't waves, it was the breeze in my tree. I lowered my face, let go of the rail with one hand, turned my back on the sun and opened my eyes. No, I wasn't at the seaside, I wasn't even on holiday. I was in my front garden, having come out to close the gate that the postman had left open.

And I was alone. Still alone.

EE Blythe

July 14: I Don't Like Cats

I don't like cats, nasty sly creatures that kill for pleasure and care for nothing but themselves.

A long time ago, in the bitter winter of 1890, a man died. He was aged 82 and separated from his wife, he lived in lodgings and begged for his living. Sometimes he was seen standing outside the family home, looking in.

On Christmas Day, he had dinner with his landlord and in the afternoon complained of pains in the chest. He went to bed alone, and in the morning it was found that he had died.

At the inquest, his wife, who, it said, did not seem to regret the death in any way, alleged her husband said wicked things about her. That he had called out "Mew", and told passers-by, "She keeps forty cats". When questioned, she said she kept two.

The doctor was of the opinion that death was accelerated by the cold weather and the jury agreed.

Not me. Perhaps there were other reasons for the separation, but I suspect that the cats drove him out, denied him a comfortable life in his own home.

Cats killed my great-great-grandfather. It's not surprising I dislike them.

Christine Hancock

July 15: The School Run

That was odd, thought Amed, journeying to the study centre one day. He was reading the latest Marvel comic, *Heroes of the Western Empire* (print version of course, actually hand-delivered to his door by courier, how super hip was that?), but had glanced up when his hydrogen-powered, autonomous cab slowed suddenly - quite unexpectedly. Crossing the street was a man wearing very short, flappy trousers and a thin vest top.

Apart from it being very inconsiderate to step into the path of a vehicle, it was highly unusual to see anyone out on the streets at seven in the morning; it was already 25 degrees. This guy was moving at more than walking pace, Amed thought; it was what used to be called jogging. And he must have been over fifty.

For some reason, Amed could not get the image of the man out of his head. It was not actually illegal for the elderly to venture out, but it was considered a serious affront, offending the younger, responsible, deserving members of society. The guilty generation were expected to keep a pretty low profile and hope they were not investigated under the ecocide laws for past collusion or wilful neglect.

The young were in charge now, dealing with the consequences of their parents' and grandparents' lack of vision and action. For decades they had selfishly squandered the Earth's dwindling resources and continued spewing climate-changing toxic gases into the atmosphere; they had simply buried their heads in the sand. The Gaia Revolutions, which had spread across the entire globe during the 2040s, were the turning point. Young people had wrenched control from complacent governments and corrupt regimes. The over-50s were now barred from voting, dozens of politicians, business leaders and dictators were safely incarcerated, or had been executed. The present was not one that Amed's generation would have chosen, but the future was in safe hands.

The cab smoothly recovered its speed and continued its journey. Amed smiled and returned to his reading. **Steve Redshaw**

July 16: Loving The Robot

"Do you still love me?" She sounded hysterical.

"Do you still love me?" She sounded more hysterical.

"Do you still love me?" She sounded even more hysterical.

Then she exploded.

Eric took a sip from his drink and said, "Told you. This robot is not built to cope with emotions."

Gerald said, "But I did as you said. I flooded it with dramatic scenes from soaps."

Rosa said, "That could be it. You may have overloaded it."

Carol said, "I don't think so. I think you made it too dramatic. I think you have made the first drama queen robot."

Eric said, "Okay, let's go with that. All we need to do is tone her down a bit, so she doesn't explode."

Gerald worked all week on the robot and the following Monday he presented the result.

The robot said, "Do you still love me?" It seemed a bit hysterical.

It said, again, "Do you still love me?" It seemed more hysterical.

It said, again, "Do you still love me?" It seemed even more hysterical.

But this time it sounded a bit slurred.

It said, again, "Do you still love me?" It sounded very slurred.

Rosa said, "It's melting. Look, in the middle."

Eric took a sip from his drink, and said, "Told you. This robot is not built to be dramatic."

Gerald said, "But I did as you said. I took her along to the 'Writing for Therapy' group'."

Rosa said, "That could be it. You may have overloaded it."

Carol said, "I don't think so. I think you made it very angry."

Eric said, "Okay. Let's go with that. All we need to do is tone her down a little, so she doesn't get too angry."

Gerald worked on the robot all week and the following Monday he presented the result. The robot said, "Do you still love me?" It sounded angry and hysterical.

It said, again, "Do you still love me?" It sounded more angry and hysterical.

It said, "Did you ever love me?" It sounded even more angry and hysterical.

Then, somehow, it both melted and exploded.

Eric took a sip from his drink, and said "Told you..."

Gerald stood up and shouted, "I've had enough of this. Make your own robot."

Eric sat up in his chair. "That was perfect. Say that again. You got the expression just right for the robot. Now, if we..."

Gerald picked up part of an arm from the robot and threw it at Eric.

Eric said, "Why did you do that?" He sounded hurt.

Gerald said, "That was perfect. Say that again..."

Carol interrupted, "It's a robot. Why would anyone love a robot?"

Peter Maudsley

July 17: The Lucky-Lucky Man

In your town, in a suburb, not far from the biggest cherry tree on the verge, lived the neighbour. He was in his living room. His front gate clanged open and scraped his asphalt path in a way that meant only one thing. Peering through the net curtains, the neighbour was so surprised to see the Lucky-Lucky man; easily forty, with nineties sideburns and an old Val Doonican cardigan.

Back again? Especially after all the coverage in the local and national papers?

"I got two steaks today, Mr Kavanagh. Fresh. It's a quid each." They were large, shrink-wrapped with the labels ripped off.

The neighbour said, "What are you playing at? I thought you'd be long gone!"

"My business, my business," he murmured in reply, unsatisfactorily. "Mister, do you want these steaks or not?"

"I'm so surprised to see you. You haven't been round in six weeks or so."

"I've been busy sorting everything out."

"It's such an obvious question." The neighbour changed trains of thought. "We called you the Lucky-Lucky man only because you fortuitously got stuff we might want to buy but now you really are lucky. A two million pound lottery win buys a lot of steaks."

Again, the cardigan caught the neighbour's attention.

He could easily afford a new one, thought the neighbour.

"Why are you still doing this now? Kids stole the cash? You can't need me to help you out any more."

Tucking the steaks under his arm and exposing a new Rolex, the Lucky-Lucky Man seemed about to say something.

Without a sound, he turned around and walked away.

Chris Wright

July 18: Esme And George

George waved her off at the station. Esme was on her way to London to see her sister, take in a show, visit a chic coffee shop, inhale the glorious stench of the city, and luxuriate in being cosmopolitan for a couple of days.

She found a seat and waved - *Railway Children*-style - at her husband as the train inched its way along the platform. Then she was gone and George felt strangely exhilarated by his temporary independence.

He'd been planning what he would do with the absence for ages. He could watch that film he'd been longing to see, but which Esme didn't fancy. He could eat his microwave meal in front of the telly, with his feet up on the coffee table. He could chat, innocently, to Paula, his newly-single neighbour, who liked to wander about barefoot in the dusk, caressing the occasional flower and looking wistful. He could stay up until midnight drinking glasses of wine and not even set an alarm for the following morning. He was a mighty king in his own castle and there were no rules, other than those he had made himself.

But an hour into his freedom, George was starting to have regrets. Just how good was this single life? Wasn't it a bit quiet around here? They don't use the phrase 'my other half' without good reason. He felt like half a person, half-living, half-experiencing real life, a shadow of himself, shoved down out of sight. He felt like life had stopped, his battery had run out.

There was so much time in the day, so many things he could be doing, but he didn't feel like doing any of them. He realised his love for Esme was something so fundamental to his life, that he was an incomplete thing without her around. He was bereft, utterly, and knew there was no happiness but the happiness he found sharing his ordinary life with the extraordinary Esme. And it wasn't even half a life without her, it was no life at all. It was the longest love affair he'd ever had, and he couldn't exist without it. He was crushed, so down with romance.

John Howes

July 19: Ferdinand

The young man paced up and down the corridor, his heart pounding. Other young men, all who looked quite similar to him, were practising their lines or warming up their voices. But this young man was struggling to breathe.

"Ferdinand Oz!" His name had been called. It was his turn. But his legs wouldn't move. His parents had wanted a longer first name for their only child, to balance out how short the surname Oz was. They'd wanted a name with impact. It had impact all right.

"Ferdinand Oz," he'd heard over and over. "With a name like that you'll be in showbusiness."

And here he was. Waiting in the wings of the theatre, about to audition for yet another starring role in yet another hit musical.

"Acting is extremely competitive," he'd been warned. But he'd sailed through every step of the way. This belief everyone seems to have that he was destined for show business had somehow opened doors for him in the most incredible way.

It was a belief that had certainly messed with his head. He'd never quite managed to kick a ball around a pitch, despite how much he loved football, but he'd excelled at dancing and singing. He'd been top of his class at RADA.

"Ferdinand Oz!" the voice called again, summoning him to the stage.

He knew his heart wasn't in it. The joke had gone on for too long. He wasn't happy.

Ferdinand secretly loved maths. He'd joined the maths club at school, praying that his arty friends would never find out. He was often playing maths games online at night, away from prying eyes.

But what if they did find out? He was now twenty-four. Wasn't it time he followed his dreams?

"I want to be an accountant!" he yelled out, relishing in the liberation of finally being honest.

Ferdinand threw off his sparkly jacket and raced out of the theatre. Enough was enough. His life began today.   **Lindsay Woodward**

July 20: Where Do You Go To, My Lovely?

Look into my eyes...

Dear Peter,

Meet me at our usual place, for lunch, this Friday?

Much love, Marie-Claire

The hand-written note from her brought on a flood of emotions he thought he buried years ago. It was twenty years since they had last spoken, but her getting in touch wasn't a complete surprise. He'd read in the newspapers that her millionaire husband – an industrialist from the Savoie – had died in a car crash on the treacherous D902 between Morzine and Marnaz.

The usual place was Il Tinello, their favourite Italian restaurant in Juan Les Pins. He decided to make a short holiday of it. He needed a break from the bank in Zurich. Besides, his latest toy, a new electric-blue Renault Alpine A110, needed exercising.

The drive from Switzerland to the French Riviera was exhilarating and he checked into the Hotel Belle Rives at 4pm on the Wednesday, tired but filled with anticipation. Thursday came and went with a mixture of swimming, sun-bathing and walking around their old haunts. Evening fell, and after a light dinner and an early night, he felt ready to face her.

Friday dawned. A mixture of nervous excitement and morbid curiosity washed over him as he walked to the restaurant. He hadn't been there long when he saw her crossing the promenade, wearing a peppermint green Balmain summer dress. She had been alluring at 17, stunning at 23, but at 45 she was beyond compare. Men and women alike looked twice as she walked up the restaurant's steps.

"Hello Pietro," she said. Nobody had called him that since they had been children together in Naples.

"I thought you'd gone and forgotten me forever," he replied.

"How can I forget you? I see you every night when I'm alone in my bed."

Simon Parker

July 21: My Favourite View

As I write, there is a painting of my favourite view. In fact, it often appears high on many lists of Britain's favourite view. It is Wastwater in the Lake District. The lake is the deepest in the country and the view looks towards some of England's highest peaks.

I have been here many times and the picture is full of memories. One of our first visits was when we stayed in a National Trust cottage at the foot of the lake, and this view or a similar one was just a short walk away, an after-dinner stroll.

On the right are The Screes, a steep slope of loose rock. There is a path, but dangerous, ever moving. From where we stayed there was a long but easy walk to the top, fantastic views. That day was hot, my husband wore shorts and was badly sunburnt, the baby on his back had a hat and survived the experience.

Beyond the ridge lies Eskdale, a gentler valley where we have often stayed, at a pub in Boot, an appropriate name in an area where the only entertainment is walking. There is a path, a copse road, between Eskdale and Wasdale; we have walked it many times, in every type of weather.

The mountain on the left is Yewbarrow. The path from this side runs straight up a narrow edge, no deviations, a steady slog, only a stile an excuse to stop and admire the view. Bear to the left and you reach a saddle, a place for a picnic if the weather is kind, then continue to Red Pike, one of two of that name. You could continue, because this is the start of a horseshoe of peaks. We never did. Not enough time, or energy, although we managed several on different occasions, from Wasdale Head.

This place is civilisation in these wilds, hardly a village: a hotel, a tiny church - Saint Olaf's – this is Viking country, and a National Trust campsite. The hotel has a bar, Ritson's, named for a famous climber of the area. The walls are covered with old black and white photographs of rugged rocks and men with ropes. A good place for a pint of local ale and perhaps lunch. Many a time we have sheltered here from rain.

Stone flagstones mean there is no need to remove your walking boots.

Next to the bar is a small shop, The Barn Door. It sells outdoor equipment, boots and rucksacks, technical books on climbing and all the Wainwright volumes – we have the full set, buying a new one on each visit. It also caters for the campsite, coffee and breakfast cereal and replacement tent pegs. And Kendal Mint Cake, my favourite food, but only allowed when I have climbed a mountain!

Towering above Wasdale Head, and the end of the horseshoe, is Great Gable. That's the mountain in the centre of the picture, its head in the sun. It was sunny the day we climbed it, at two thousand, nine hundred and forty-nine feet, one of the tallest in the area. It was at the end of a week's holiday, longer than the usual weekend, so we had time to build up our strength. A great achievement.

Perhaps if we had stayed longer, we would have made it to the top of Scafell Pike, tallest peak in England. I don't suppose I ever will now, but you never know.

There has to be something left to strive for. It is not in the picture, it hides, dark and menacing behind the other hills. Perhaps I will conquer it, and if I do, it will provide me with more memories.

I'll need a new picture though.

Christine Hancock

July 22: Lost

According to some folk, you can see five counties from up here. On a fine day, that is.

Well, I've been up here more times than I care to remember, and I've only ever seen the one I'm standing in.

Great view, though, isn't it? That's the new reservoir down there. Though it's been a good few years since it were new. I remember that reservoir when it were a bog. There were a right how-dya-do when they flooded that valley. Farmers complained, of course, despite the compensation. Nothing new about that.

Have you ever met a happy farmer? I haven't. I've had a stick waved at me many a time. And some of 'em take the footpath signs off the stiles, or turn 'em round so that they point in the wrong direction. That's worse. You can walk a mile or more without realising you're going the wrong way.

There were that time I got lost in Blackmoor Forest. Wandered round for hours getting more and more lost.

We'd had a lot of rain and there were puddles and mud everywhere. Well, I came to this great patch of mud and I had no alternative but to walk straight through it, but it got worse in the middle, just like slurry, and I went in right over the top of my wellie boots. Shows you how deep it was.

Well, I were standing there, sinking in deeper and deeper, trying to extricate myself, when along the path comes this chap on a unicycle. I thought I must be having a nightmare, but he were real all right.

He gets off his bike and says, "Which way is it to the nearest railway station?"

I says, "What?! You're asking me to tell you the way to the railway station and you can see me stuck here in this predicament. You come and help me out, then maybe I'll tell you."

So he got a long worm-eaten stick out of the undergrowth and held it out for me to get hold of. The end kept breaking off it, but, after a lot of slithering around, he eventually pulled me out, all covered in mud.

"Now," I says. "If I knew the way to a railway station I'd tell you, but I'm as lost as you are. Why don't we go back the way you've come, then we'll know where we are?"

"I can't go back there," he says.

"Why not?" I says. "We can't both stay here, and it'll be dark in half an hour."

"I'm in a spot of trouble," he says.

"What sort of trouble?"

"My boss has accused me of something I didn't do, and he's set the police on me."

"Well, if you didn't do it, you've got nothing to worry about," I says. "Why don't you go back and explain your side of the situation?"

So then he started this long rigmarole about how he worked as a trick cyclist in a touring circus, and he also worked in the ticket booth before the show, and how his boss had accused him of fiddling the money and had called the cops, so he'd grabbed his unicycle, which he kept handy in the ticket office, and sped off into the woods, where the police car couldn't go.

So, here we were in Blackmoor Forest, cops on his trail, both of us lost and night coming on.

Well, just as we were looking around for somewhere to cosy down for the night, we saw lights coming towards us. I were right glad to see 'em, but this trick cyclist bloke wasn't so keen because it turned out to be his boss and a couple of coppers.

They clapped the handcuffs on him there and then and led him off.

And they took me along, too, as an accomplice.

So that's how I got out of the woods.

Wendy Goulstone

July 23: The Haunted Hotel

I do murder mysteries. Because I do not drive, I am taken all over the country to play characters. This particular weekend, it is a hotel in Torquay. Shades of *Fawlty Towers*. I am playing a Russian medium. In the plot, the hotel is haunted. We stop first at a tatty little hotel. This is where we will sleep, up three flights of stairs. No lifts, of course, to leave our stuff. Then onto our destination. Our boss goes to the reception to talk to the manager where we are shown our rehearsal room. It's up three flights of stairs and is an ironing cupboard. There are eight of us actors, I kid you not. Then it's back down to put our characters' names on tables.

We find we have 49 guests in half the dining room! Then back up the stairs to rehearse and get costumed up. At 7.30pm, we go into the dining room to find the manager has removed all our names from the tables and put all of us together on a table outside the kitchen doors. He tells us we must eat in shifts. Unbelievable.

Our way of working is to go from table to table making sure the guests know who we are and what is happening. Now we get to the bit where I announce I am a real medium and that I will hold a seance. I light my candle and ask for the lights to be switched off and for silence while I contact the spirit. But of course half the room are still being served and chatting and the waiters are walking about.

After three attempts, I give up. There is a loud scream and a body falls into the room. Then, with our guests, we go up to the bar and they try to work out who does what to whom. Our policeman comes and reads a report, and one of us is arrested. A prize is won by the best answer. We go up to the cupboard to get changed before walking back to our first hotel to climb the three flights to go to bed. I do not know why the manager disliked us so much unless it was because we made him more work. Needless to say, we never went there again.

Ruth Hughes

July 24: The Gift Token

The wind was getting up as I followed five others and clambered into the basket. Immediately the gas ignited and fired up with a deafening roar as the basket rocked like a racehorse, impatient to be let loose. I gripped the side, afraid to join the conversation which was going on behind me: shrieks of laughter, joyous enthusiasm for their first flight in a hot air balloon. It was my first time too, but I'd never asked for this. The trip was a gift token, given to me at Christmas, with a gesture of pure love. I had to accept.

The basket lurched, the fire roared again and we were being dragged along the ground until suddenly the whole party of us lifted up and up with a swoosh and a feeling of being elevated without the safe confines of four lift walls. Cries of sheer delight pierced my shroud of terror.

Then the basket sort of calmed down, drifted like a bubble in the warm summer air. We hung there suspended. My companions murmured and pointed out various landmarks, the fields of Rugby School, St. Cross Hospital, and we floated on – Daventry Reservoir passed below but we were climbing higher, and higher... I felt totally helpless. I was a pigeon clutched in the claws of a giant eagle. At any moment the great horny beak would come down and tear into my flesh.

Perhaps I fainted because the next thing I knew we were falling quite rapidly. Those behind me were shrieking. Trees came into focus, the tops of trees, even the leaves, telegraph wires, and chimneys. Then we were gliding in a downwards sweep towards open farmland where a tractor was so close the driver looked upwards and shouted at us in alarm. A horrible scraping sound thundered in our ears as the basket hit the ground. We were hauled along by the balloon in a ridiculous, almost comic limp to a final resting place in a blackthorn hedge. It was over.

Theresa Le Flem

July 25: Lavinia And Brian

Once upon a time there was a princess called Lavinia. She wanted to be a sorceress. The Court Magician arranged for her training and found her a familiar: a talking frog called Brian. Looking through Brian's eyes was tricky at first, but she improved and became a Grade 3 sorceress.

One day, Lavinia was out with Brian in her pocket. Suddenly her bodyguards were ambushed by an evil wizard who paralysed them with his wand and imprisoned her in a cell in his tower. However Caz the wizard had not checked her pockets.

Brian hopped through the bars of her cell and went exploring. He found the antechamber to Caz's lab. He had left one of his spell books open. Brian looked at it so Lavinia could read it. Two of his spells looked useful, but could a Grade 3 sorceress use them?

Lavinia had to try.

The first spell bent the bars of the cell far enough for her to get out, but she thought she should stop Caz from following them. Her attempt to fill the antechamber with thorns didn't quite work: the spell filled the room with green jelly instead. That would do. She unbarred the main door and left, just as the King's search party arrived.

Starving the wizard out would have taken time, especially with all that jelly to eat, but three days later the tower suddenly disintegrated in a pile of dust. Except for the jelly. The Court Magician said the jelly had survived disintegration because it was magically created.

Lavinia and Brian became Best Friends. He always refused politely but firmly to be kissed, saying he was afraid he might turn into a prince.

Lavinia couldn't argue with that. He had always been very happy being a frog.

Jim Hicks

July 26: Where Is Safe?

"Run, Run, *Run!*"

When a policeman tells you to run, you do just that. I turned on my heels and sprinted before my brain could even catch up.

Seconds later, I remembered that I wasn't alone. My parents were with me, and there was no way they were going to be able to run as fast as I could. I turned back and grabbed my mom's arm to help her along.

That's when it hit me. Where could we run to? We didn't know what the threat was. We had just been told to run. When you don't know what the threat is, how do you know where safe is?

All we could fathom was that we had to run in the opposite direction from where the policeman was. We had to get as far away from him as possible.

We reached the start of Southwark bridge in the heart of London and, without hesitation, we began to run across it. Police boats were soaring down the Thames, helicopters were above us, and flashing lights were everywhere. Whatever was going on, it was serious.

My mom later described the scene as a war zone. It felt just like that. Dark, fearful and never ending.

My phone began ringing in my bag. I could feel the vibrations against my hip. I wanted to answer it. I assumed it would be my husband. We were supposed to meet him in the pub. He was less than half a mile away from us, but behind that policeman. He was trapped somewhere in the centre of whatever this threat was.

I couldn't stop, though. Images of someone with a knife or a gun flashed through my mind. They could be chasing us. We could literally be on the verge of losing our lives. We couldn't stop. At the other side of the bridge we saw a small crowd of people who seemed as afraid and bewildered as we were. As we approached them, we slowed down. We were running out of breath, and we needed to see if they had any clue what was happening.

"I heard someone was stabbed," one person said.

"I heard a gunshot," another detailed.

My parents told them about how we'd been ordered to run while I scrambled for my phone in my bag.

The missed call was from my husband, just as I had expected. I quickly called him back.

"When I call, answer your phone!" he snapped at me.

"I couldn't!" I yelled back. "The police told us to run. We were running. I couldn't answer."

"Okay," he said, backing down. "Are you all right? I was so worried. When you didn't answer… I've never been so scared."

"Something's going on, but we don't know what. These people are saying they've heard gunshots."

"I've got it on the news now. I'm back in our hotel room."

"We can't get back to the hotel. They roads are all blocked."

"You couldn't anyway. I'm locked in. They've locked us in. Nobody can get out and nobody can get in. Someone has been running people over. You need to get to safety. Where are you?"

"At the end of Southwark Bridge."

"You need to get off the road. Get away from the road now!"

"Someone's been running people over!" I told the group. "My husband's got it on the news. We need to get to safety. We can't get back to the hotel."

"Call me back when you're away from the road," my husband said.

"I will do. I love you."

"I love you too."

I shoved my phone back in my bag and I took in our surroundings.

The roads were gridlocked. The tube lines had all been closed. Streets were blocked off. All we had were our feet and our phones, with the batteries swiftly losing charge.

It was half past ten on a Saturday night in Central London. We were caught up in the middle of a Terrorist Attack. We had no way of knowing what was happening, where was safe and whether we'd survive.

My brain began acting in the strangest of ways. I stopped being able to process the most basic of things, and suddenly all I could think of was planning how to get myself and my parents away from the road, away from the threat and somewhere safe for us to stay until all of this was resolved.

The dread of what lay ahead burned inside of me and I wanted to cry, but I couldn't. All that mattered now was survival. As all other thoughts faded away, I looked at my parents and we marched on.

Lindsay Woodward

July 27: The Death Of Romance

The room is tidy and so light and airy. Cheerful, some would say, except rooms are objects and objects don't feel – and I'm not cheerful. Sometimes I feel as if I'm an object. It's not right. Not right at all. He treats me like an object most of the time. A robot.

His newspaper rustles. The only sound. Not even a clock. That relentless tick-tock, tick-tock – the sound of boredom. Tick-tock: the march of time, no going back, step by step. Towards death. With him.

Another rustle. "Another lorry stuck under that bridge again. Fourth time this year."

"Fifth." I like correcting him. I enjoy being right, correcting someone who's always so bloody (oops, I swore!) self-sure – always. Because he's a man? The Head of the Household. The Provider. The Decider. The Tyrant.

"M6 was blocked again. Eight hours yesterday. Thank God I chose the other way. Lucky there."

He smirks and raises his head. Not much hair loss there. Quite presentable really, though thank God he doesn't present himself to me so much these days.

"I saw a rat again last night when I got back. Shot off under next door's fence. You've been throwing bread out for the birds again. Back lawn was covered in the stuff. Even in the dark. I'll have next door complaining if you don't stop."

"I like to see the birds. It's something to do. I like their company."

"You'll have rats for company if you don't watch out."

What's wrong with her? he thought.

Chris Rowe

July 28: Cats' Rules In The Garden

Rule One: Cats are allowed in my garden as long as I can't see them. What's out of sight is out of mind and won't creep me out.

Rule Two: Cats shall pass through my garden in minimum time. If my greyhound is about, then, as fast as felinely possible, finally running up my fence like a squirrel.

Rule Three: Cats should beware my children with their toy guns. I have asked them not to shoot cats with catapults or BB guns but have said nothing about Nerf™ guns, water pistols or paintball guns.

Rule Four: Cats *are not* to leave droppings in my garden, even if buried. We don't want your treasure and we know where you live. Also don't dig up my guinea pigs' graves again.

Rule Five: Do not sniff my lilies if they are in bloom. You have been warned and I keep them in the centre bed next to the cat mint.

Rule Six: Do not make any noise in my garden or in its vicinity. You might think you're singing, I might think next-door's are starving their baby.

Rule Seven: You can help yourself to any rats, mice, voles and definitely moles but birds are off your menu. Pigeons can be considered flying rats for the purposes of this rule. Stay away from the frogs in my pond. Squirrels in trees are safe anyway.

Rule Eight: House cats are the best cats. Roaming, ranging ones are the worst. On film cats are great: on YouTube, in museums or featured in amusing adverts – or best of all snug in my neighbours' houses. If you come into my garden you are just a visitor.

Rule Nine: Cats obeying these rules will be tolerated, be threatened with nothing worse than half a cup of clean water and will even be allowed to use the hedgehog's doorway.

By order.

Chris Wright F.I.D.O.

July 29: John-John

It was my first week at the hospital and John-John was my mentor. He was going to show me things, show me the ropes. Here was an old man, standing before me now, an old man before his time. His eyes were ringed with lines and then ringed again, the flesh sagging in against itself and in shadow, the irises a pale watery grey; sparse hair receding on top and swept back into nothing. With a permanent aroma of stale tobacco. The smell not unpleasant but telling, telling of bachelorhood and a bedsit room somewhere in Hampstead. The shirt cuffs frayed.

"Costs a fair bit to live round here, matey."

He took home less than 900 a month, plus the overtime. But he had to live round here. He was a hospital porter at the Royal Free, Hampstead. Mondays to Saturdays.

"Only three hours on Saturdays." And he laughed a dry wheezed laugh. "Don't do much Saturdays, just collect the boxes, the medical boxes from each ward in the hospital. All twelve floors. Don't do the bags or anything."

The ubiquitous bags. These were shiny, hard-to-hold plastic bags delivered to the back door of the Porters' room from the Pharmacist and delivered by hand to the ward and then passed on to patients. Every day except Sundays.

John-John they called him, the hospital porter.

"Been here 22 years all told - since it opened. Oh, that was a grand affair, Princess Margaret no less, and consultants lined up like dominoes. We cleared away caviar and honeyed rolls if I remember right."

John-John, shoulders hunched in a shabby white coat, unbuttoned, stiff with grime. Trousers unruly and creased. Shuffling along the clean-swept endless corridors. A shuffling gait as if even the effort of lifting his feet in unison was beyond him. As if even the neurons and synapse had surrendered in defeat to him. A face forever old at 50. Skin grey and parched of sunlight. But a man not without the gift of friendship; a wave of his hand was like a papal dispensation. He was giving me my initiation.

"It's only ten now but nothing comes in till eleven. Go get yourself a tea break. Me? I'm making myself scarce."

And he would, perching himself outside in an alcove, on the twelfth floor, by the lift bay, huddled from the draft. Leaning in against the stone work. Inhaling on a hand-rolled cigarette, palm cupped against the wind. Eyes ever watchful for the boxes. Of medium height, not an ounce of fat on this man but quiet, ever-present anxiety in his eyes. This man held the keys. The keys to the lift shaft. This man decided the speeds at which those ward boxes were delivered. Or not. They ascended or descended at his will. Delivering the boxes well meant you got to go home early. And John-John was a past master.

At first as the days melded into my first week, I admired and envied his nonchalance. His cool, his lack of concern for time pressures. Later I realised this was illusionary. John-John was a person ground into and part of the structure. His job was to preserve that structure as best he could. It was a battle. Every day was a battle. A battle to deliver the boxes and go home early.

Somewhere else in this building, hearts were being exchanged by gloved hands wet with blood, babies were struggling for their first gasps of air, stored cadavers slowly stiffening with rigor mortis but our job was to deliver the boxes and get home early.

And that was John-John's modus operandi for the entire day. How to deliver the minimum of boxes to satisfy demand and gain the maximum time for himself. As the weeks progressed, he showed me the various nooks and crannies that would evade the casual eye. How to amend a timesheet to glean an additional quarter of an hour of time served. When best to go to the canteen.

I was even allowed to unload myself. Twice a day lorries would arrive in the backyard with sealed cardboard boxes. Small lightweight ones inevitably bound for pharmacy. And then endless boxes of Teacher's Whisky, distilled water and Guinness. The hospital seemed to flow around water and alcohol.

By week three, I sort of understood the hidden codes and practices of portering. And then John-John disappeared. He simply didn't come in. And no one knew why. A mild curiosity permeated the porters' room. John-John, not a man to ever miss a day's work, no longer here. A junior porter took over the intricacies of the lift shaft and despatch of boxes. And a marked improvement in delivery ensued.

So much so that I feared for John-John's return. How would he explain it? But I needn't have worried. John-John had died in his bedsit and, single man that he was, hadn't been discovered for three weeks. I went to the funeral, standing with three others, including his sister who'd come over from Ireland to collect anything valuable. The priest spoke of endless selfless years of service to the community and the gaping loss to the hospital.

We brought our own drinks in the snug bar and the sister spoke of those bright blue eyes he had as a child. And a fine tenor voice. Back at the hospital things more or less returned to normal. This was a place immune to loss and bereavement but I couldn't help feeling, or rather smelling, as I trundled empty clanking beds across pristine floors, that occasional stale aroma of frayed cuffs, too-long-worn trousers and stale tobacco. As if his aura had sunk itself into those walls. The only remaining legacy of John-John, my one-time mentor.

Oh and I never mentioned those secret hiding places. They were his alone. Until others discovered them.

Simon Grenville

July 30: The Hatchling

The day had started out much the same way as every morning - first feed the hens, then collect the eggs. This time, there was a strange little purple egg with yellow splashes on its shell. I decided to put it in the incubator with the batch I was going to hatch.

Two weeks later, I came down to find a curious little purple creature crawling round the incubator. I picked him up and set him on the palm of my hand. He made little keening noises. I knew he was hungry. After much trial and error, I discovered he liked egg and chips best but would eat almost anything.

There were yellow splashes on his purple skin. I called him Murple. He seemed to like it as a name. He would wrap his tail around my wrist while I stroked under his chin and down his back. He had beautiful little wings folded on his sides and claws on his feet that he used to hold on with. He had swirly eyes of glorious emerald green flecked with gold and his little nostrils puffed out smoke. In a week or two, they puffed out their first fire.

He was very careful not to set anything on fire. He would now perch on my shoulder as he got bigger and croon into my ear; it was blissful. He began to test out his wings, zooming round me when we went outside. It was probably on the sixth week when, one fine day, he zoomed off and I never saw him again.

You cannot imagine the loneliness and sense of loss I felt without him. I hope he is well and happy and, who knows, maybe one day I shall find another purple egg to hatch.

Ruth Hughes

July 31: Pemberton

Pemberton. Pen, to his family and friends. He completed forms as Pen, his bank card said Pen, even to the taxman he was Pen. But he knew he was Pemberton.

"Pen!" Sal was gently poking him. "You're not hearing a word I'm saying." He looked into her huge brown eyes, and grinned. It had been a lucky day when he'd stumbled across her. Literally.

It had been at a festival. Not a big one with megastars helicoptering in and out for a twenty minute stint on stage. No. Small, informal, friendly, very 'new age'. Watching a barn owl quartering a nearby field he'd been walking along, beer in hand, when he'd caught his foot under something, and fallen across a small body, emptying his glass all over the said small body, as he landed. He lay still, winded, and judging by the loud 'Oooff' that had come from the body, the child was winded too. If not crushed! Realization brought him swiftly to his feet.

She wasn't a child, she was just 'petite'. She laughed as she wrung out her hair, and wiped her face. Their eyes met, music filled the air, and they melted into each other. Not quite, but close. She wasn't angry with him, which he thought was a miracle, and when she stopped laughing they'd exchanged names. She said her name was Sal. Short for Salvia.

"It's the herb Sage, so you can guess what my parents are like. I'm just lucky they didn't call me Moonbeam or Solstice!" And he told her he was Pen, short for Pemberton, which was indirectly his grandfather's fault.

They had kept in touch while they both finished university courses, and by then he'd known he didn't want to be so far away from her ever again. Luckily she'd felt the same.

"Pen! What's up with you today?" He laughed. But his eyes kept straying across the camping field to a small maroon and dove-grey caravan.

"It's the penalty of having hippy parents," Sal said softly, looking in the same direction. At the old Pemberton caravan.　　　　**EE Blythe**

August

.

August 1: The Worst Night Of My Life

The missus, she's a light-sleeper, she heard it first, the crackle, the cries, poked me in the ribs.

"Harry", she says, "Wake up! Wake up!"

"Wha'? Wha'? Go to sleep."

"Harry!" And another dig in the ribs. "Hear that? There's summat going on. Harry, get up and see what's up."

And she pushed me out of bed with a thud. So I staggered to the window, muttering and grumbling. There were flashes of light bouncing off the house across the road and folks in the street shouting. They were rushing about everywhere, some with buckets, some, carrying bags and babbies, making off in the opposite direction.

"Make haste! Bring that bucket. Here, give it me. Come on. Har over." That were Matt from next-door-but-one, running about v nightshirt on.

"Never mind the bucket. Get the kids out." That were his wi' takes in washing.

"Where's Alice? Matthew, hold the babby while I find / Where are you?"

Alice is right behind her, holding a little 'un by the scruf

"I'm here, Mam. I don't like it, Mam. I don't wan! Mam."

"Gerr off me," screams the little 'un, trying to bre babby's wailing for its mother.

And Matt's still yelling, "The roof's on fire! Bring a _ooks we're

I says, "Eh, get up quick, woman. There's sumr like flames coming from next door. We'd better cinders."

My missus is out of bed now, pushing me out ut to death.

"Harry!" she screams in my ear. "Harry! \ Quick, quick! Hurry up!" More shouts from the ill yelling for a

Matt's wife is trying to hold on to the kids bucket.

"You're wasting your time," she screams. "It's too late. We'll burn to death."

"Harry! Hurry up, Harry, you great mollykin. We've got to get out."

"My life savings are up in the attic," I says. "I'm not going without my money."

"Well, I'm going, if you're not. Where's me shoes? I can't find me shoes. Where's me shoes?"

"Never mind your shoes. Get your clobber on, quick." But she's found her shoes under the bed and is struggling to put 'em on.

"I'm off," she says, and she's trying to drag me downstairs, but I nip up the ladder quick to get me money out of its hiding place. I'm fumbling with the lock, but I drop the key and can't find it.

When I'm down in the street, thatch of next door was ablaze already, timbers catching. We could have been dead if we hadn't woke up. My missus is helping Matt's wife to grab the kids.

Matt shouts at his missus, "Take the nippers and go to my mother's."

But her says, "She's got the plague. I'm not going there. Be quiet, ducky. Alice, hold onto my skirt and don't let go. Come on, Matt. I can't cope with the kids on my own, and carry a bag as well."

Next door was now blazing. It would be ours next.

The wind was driving the flames down the street from the ehouse. So we made off like a shot down Pudding Lane in the other tion. Went to me sister's. Her husband wasn't too pleased.

at geyser wrote it all down of course, you know the one, him well known by all the loose women within ten miles of here. I buried his cheese in the garden before he scarpered. I don't ever dug it up again. Pepys, Samuel Pepys, that's who it was.

Wendy Goulstone

August 2: Unity Mitford In Rugby

Some of these chips are too greasy, but I don't care. I'm sitting in a cold kitchen in Winfield Street in a backwater called Rugby. They've left up the blackout curtains, even in the day. The peasants.

I'd rather be here than out in the town though, with people staring and pointing at the fallen aristocracy. I don't mind Frank and Pete. Frank is sitting opposite me with his sausage in batter, Pete - his crutches leaning against the table - prefers a bit of fish. He's a darling, nice to everyone, and his sketching is better than mine. They love him at the art college.

They're a bit suspicious of me tagging along but these simple working class boys are good for me. My head aches a bit and I keep getting dizzy. The bullet's still in there and they say it'll kill me one day, but I'm not bothered.

Frank eyes me questioningly as if he's about to say something important.

"What was he like, then?"

"What was who like?" I reply, mischievously.

"You know who I mean," says Frank. "Adolf, the Fuhrer."

"How should I know? I barely knew him," I lie, thinking back to those wondrous afternoons in the Osteria Bavaria in Munich, waiting at my table, day after day for him to come in. Finally, he had beckoned me over and our friendship had begun, I'd been drawn in to his inner circle, become a confidante, fallen for this gallant, wondrous visionary and his plan for a better world. Over a hundred times we met until he told me to go home as our countries were at war.

I thought that was the end. I'd taken out the revolver given to me by the Fuhrer and shot myself in the English garden. God, I wanted to be dead but it wasn't to be, and now look at me, eating chips in this hovel, waiting for the end of the war, waiting for the end of my life.

Frank doesn't believe me. Pete gives me the benefit of the doubt, but I say nothing more. Nothing will ever change the way I feel about the Fuhrer.

I feel like I am the luckiest girl in the world. For me, he is the greatest man of all time.

*The last paragraph features the paraphrased words of Unity Mitford who spent several years in Rugby, Warwickshire from 1943 onwards. Frank, in this story, was my grandfather, Frank Howes.

John Howes

August 3: Le Tour Eiffel

I know the Eiffel Tower is an inanimate object, yet this magnificent latticework of wrought iron has a powerful hold over me. The first time I saw the tower for real in 1994, and walked up to and touched the intricate ironwork, I was transported back to an earlier time in my mind. A time I was never a part of and one that I have no personal frame of reference for. A turbulent but vivacious time for France, which people who were there talk about in hushed tones: the student protests of 1968.

Aurelie and I are lovers. I am 21, she is 19. We meet at a protest rally in Bordeaux over Easter weekend, as we choose the same shop doorway to escape the worst from the water cannon. We emerge, wet and bedraggled and form an instant bond, strengthened by learning that we both attend the same university in Paris. We hitch back to the city that evening in a Belgian truck, huddled together for warmth under an oil-stained blanket provided by the kind, old driver. We spend that night together in my top floor flat off the Place St. Sulpice. She goes back to her student residence in St. Germain only once after that, to collect her books and belongings.

We are inseparable for the next four years. We roam the city by day and night on my Vespa, meeting with other student groups, planning how to topple the three insidious evils of capitalism, consumerism and American imperialism.

It's absolute fiction of course, but whenever I see the tower, I wonder what other adventures we could have had in that ephemeral time. I still keep a Vespa in my small fleet of vehicles. Would anyone like to go for a ride?

Simon Parker

August 4: My First African Safari

I was petrified as the charging elephant was heading straight for us. It was 1997 and my first visit to South Africa. Diana, my younger sister, and I had travelled together to visit our older sister, Penny.

I was on my maiden safari, having travelled through the Phalaborwa Gate into the Kruger National Park in the north eastern provinces of Limpopo and Mpumalanga. Penny was driving. She's an experienced safari driver who has lived in the country since 1969 and knows the park well. For the safety of the animals and visitors, she kept to the stipulated park speed restrictions of fifty kmh on tar roads and forty kmh on gravel roads.

Suddenly there was a large herd of massive African elephants with several young calves. What an amazing sight.

However, nothing could have prepared me for the huge elephant tramping towards us from the left of our car. We drove slowly along the road when I saw another and yet another elephant until there was a gigantic herd of moving grey bodies lumbering towards us. Travelling in a small hired car, we were amongst enormously wonderful and obviously excitable wild animals.

This first sighting of elephants in the wild was even more impressive and certainly different in real life than on television wildlife programmes. The dark grey leading animal was considerably larger than I had imagined. A huge animal with many old fighting wounds gouged into its leathery skin, and large grey ears with notches lost in battles against its elephant enemies. The mighty beast had its long trunk tucked under and its ears flapping as it headed towards us from the left of the car, with other elephants surrounding its leader. I shot my head around and looked towards the right of the vehicle. To my horror there were even more elephants.

Help, let's go! I thought but sat in silence, terrified as there were now elephants surrounding us. I suddenly saw a small, very young calf huddled very close to what must have been its mother. Then we were in the middle of the advancing mob and had inadvertently separated the fiercely protective leader of the herd from its calf. Not a good place to find ourselves.

Silence in the car. Suddenly Penny put her foot down, and we shot forward. We needed to escape before the approaching wild elephants moved any closer. The car accelerated fast. No time for discussion. No warning. The speed limit forgotten, we were saving our lives by speeding into the distance, away from danger.

Eventually, I moved, turned around and looked. The herd of elephants were out of sight. We were safe.

"Has that happened before?" I nervously asked Penny.

"Not quite like that," Penny answered as she resumed the speed limit and headed for our campsite and safety.

We travelled for a few hours before arriving at our accommodation, a bush camp known as Shimuwini: just a small camp of fifteen cottages. There was nothing else, no shop, no café and we were surrounded by a high wire fence. It was an odd situation, another first for me as the gates locked us in for our own safety at dusk, 5.30pm, and opened at dawn, 5.30am, with wild animals wandering freely in their natural habitat outside our securely-fenced camp. We were totally isolated and had taken requirements for our self-catering stay, with the nearest small shops for basic essentials a few miles away.

Going to sleep with the sound of a roaring lion was eerily weird, unlike at home, where the wildest animals heard at night are dogs or foxes barking. There's no light pollution in the park, so it can be very, very dark in the depths of a pitch-black African night unless there's a cloudless night sky. Then the sky is lit by many more bright stars and constellations than we don't see at home.

Shimuwini is in a spectacular location by the Letaba River. There is a camouflaged wooden hide from where I watched wild animals, including a family of three elephants, two adults and a calf ambling along. Thankfully they were on the far side of the dry riverbed and safely behind a fence!

That was my first unforgettable memory of my Kruger Safari and elephant excitement. **Kate A.Harris**

August 5: Longbourn Book Club

It is a truth universally acknowledged that no one goes to a book club to talk about books, and especially not to listen.

Do you realise, Mr Bennet, said his good lady, that it has been a whole year since Lady Lucas and I set up our book group meeting in your study?

Yes. Why cannot you meet as you did formerly in the with-drawing room, for books are rarely your subject of discussion?

But one doesn't go to talk about books. One goes to talk to one's friends. And there aren't many of us. Our membership is much declining.

Calling it the Longbourn Lit-Chicks was perhaps too exclusive a title.

What would you suggest then?

The Medical Moaners? On the regrettable occasions when I have been subjected to enforced overhearing within my own study, I still have no idea of Lady Lucas's literary taste, though I am intimately acquainted with all fourteen of her ailments. And Sir William's account of his knee operation was most memorable, if somewhat gruesome. I almost looked forward to his monthly updatings.

There you are, then: one goes to book club to catch up with the news from one's friends.

But not apparently to increase one's friendship.

But Lady Lucas and I set it up. It's our club.

I observe you derive great pleasure from it, my dear. And you talk together with great animation, but that enjoyment does not apply to the rest of the group. I have never perceived your bestowing your attention upon those two attractive young ladies from Barton.

They don't say anything.

They are not allowed to: whenever Sir William invites their opinions, his good lady interrupts him with hers.

Yes. I find it distracting when she has to break off addressing me to prevent his talking to them. I mean, who are they?

They are from Barton.

Wherever that is.

Mr Bennet, deploring that the Dashwood sisters, endowed with both good sense and charming sensibility, were not quite integrated into the group, murmured

You should perhaps not have urged their membership.

We need the money.

You'd prefer their subscription. Without their attendance.

Your idea of renting a room at the Netherfield Hall Community Centre – we can't afford it. We need more members.

No need. I have spoken to Lizzy. Our son-in-law has taken pity upon me. So that I can have unimpeded access to my own study and prevent its invasion by the chosen literati of your acquaintance, Darcy will fund access to the Netherfield Hall library.

Pirouetting with joy about the room, Mrs Bennet did perhaps not fully comprehend his following words -

Darcy insists upon one stipulation: his aunt, Lady Catherine de Bourgh, a most forthright woman, must be a member. She's informed her nephew she is exceedingly fond of books and would have been an avid reader had her eyesight allowed. She intended to join Lizzy's group at Pemberly but was persuaded her energies would be better employed at Netherfield. She'll be bringing Mr Collins with her and has announced she'll be delighted to be your new chairwoman.

Chris Rowe

August 6: Suspicious Circumstances

As I walked along the road, I saw a group of youths huddled together. Given that this area was notorious for youth crime, drug dealing, shoplifting, gang fights and criminal damage, my senses were immediately alerted. I slowed down and watched for a moment.

There were five boys all dressed 'gangsta' style, trousers hanging down across their bottoms with grubby underwear on display. This fashion came out of the prison practice of removing belts and cords from trousers to stop offenders from harming themselves. When they were released, the act of rethreading the cord or replacing the belts was just too much for a young lad, so the trousers remained loosely hanging, at which point everyone knew that you had been in prison, and the 'style' became a 'badge of office'.

There they were, huddled in a group at the side of the road. As I watched I saw that one had a stick, they were all looking down and one lad was on his knees. My mind went into overdrive. He was being attacked, mugged, beaten with a stick! I was aware of loud voices, but I couldn't hear clearly what was being said.

As I got closer I heard, "Just give it a good pull, it should come out."

"Use the stick."

"It's not working with the stick!"

"Come on you muppet, pull it harder!"

"Man it's mingin. I don't want to touch it!"

They were so intent on what they were doing that they didn't notice me approaching.

"All right, lads, what's going on?" I said.

They all jumped, the stick hit the floor and they all looked guilty and scared.

"Nothing Miss." Another prison giveaway, all female workers in prison are 'Miss'.

"What sort of 'nothing' needs five of you and a stick?"

"Joe dropped his phone down the drain, Miss. We was tryin to get it out with a stick. Honest, Miss."

"Ok," I said. "Let me see."

I knelt down and saw the phone laying on the gunk down the drain. I always carried latex gloves with me to protect evidence and to protect me against whatever nasty bodily fluids were aimed at me, and now against stinking drains!

Gloves on, I knelt down and I pulled the drain cover off, then I put my hand down into the stinking goo and retrieved the phone.

"Aww, Miss, you are awesome."

I wiped it off with some steri wipes, while they replaced the drain cover. I put the phone into an evidence bag and handed it to Joe.

"Clean it up properly when you get home."

"Aww, Miss, that's sound. You're a sound coppa!"

"Well, you stay out of trouble and be safe. See you later lads."

"Yeah, cheers, Miss."

I carried on walking my beat with a smug smile on my face.

"A sound coppa."

I'll take that. I knew that those lads would be valuable allies for me in the area from then on. And they were!

Linda Slate

August 7: Live A Little

"Come on," Elena said, pulling me down the stairs. We were heading to a function room in a random bar we'd happened across in the middle of London.

"Isn't it illegal to crash a party?" I asked.

"It's exciting, that's what it is!" Elena said. As we reached the bottom of the staircase, she turned to me. "Sarah, you need to live a little."

At the entrance of the room I spotted a sign that said: "L M Tintershell Annual Corporate Party." It made me even more nervous. Corporate sounded official.

Just as I was about to share these very thoughts with Elena, I heard her say: "Hi, I'm Emma." She was heading over to a gorgeous man who was standing by the door. I couldn't believe it. He might be a Greek God but criminals should remain unseen.

"I don't think we've met," he replied with a beaming smile. "I'm Dan from Customer Services."

"Lovely to meet you," Elena purred. "I'm in Accounts."

I began to panic. I wasn't cut out for prison.

"Over in the Piccadilly office?" he asked. Elena confidently nodded in reply. "Cool. I'm based in London Bridge. Can I get you a drink?"

Elena winked at me as she followed the Greek God into the heart of the private party.

A very unexpected rush of adrenaline zipped through me. Elena was clever. Everywhere had to have an Accounts department. And I knew what offices were at this company now too.

Maybe I should live a little. This might be fun. What was the worst that could happen, after all?

I stepped through the door and stared around the function room in awe. There must have been a few hundred people in there. Who could know that many colleagues? I could get away with this.

Full of Dutch courage, I approached a couple of men. They too were very attractive. I made a mental note to Google L M Tintershell when I got home. I liked the look of it.

"Hi, I'm...Winona," I said with a smile. I'd always wanted to meet someone called Winona. "I don't think we've met before. What do you do?"

I didn't listen to their answers properly, I just noted that none of them worked in Accounts. That was all that mattered. This was my moment. I was actually going to do something totally immoral!

But before I could open my mouth, I felt a bump from behind. Like a domino effect, I fell forward into the hugely gorgeous man opposite me, which in turn sent his pint of Guinness flying into the air, and then splashing all over a slightly older man that just happened to be standing nearby.

"Sorry!" I said as he turned to me with anger. A weird silence seemed to grasp the air around us. The music was still pumping away in the background, but I barely noticed it against the tension immediately suffocating me.

"How much have you had to drink?" the now very wet man asked, quite sternly. The Guinness was actually dripping off him.

"Someone pushed into me," I argued, deliberately avoiding his question. This was far from the first bar we'd frequented that evening.

"I know we're all meant to be enjoying ourselves tonight, but I specifically asked that no one get too drunk."

"I didn't mean to," I said.

"How am I meant to enjoy the evening now, all soaking wet?"

"I could get you some toilet roll?" I offered.

It felt as if every pair of eyes in the room were watching me.

"Who are you?" he asked with a big booming voice.

"I'm... Winona," I replied quietly. "I work in Accounts."

"I didn"t know we had a Winona working in Accounts," he said.

"Who are you?" I squeaked, trying to prove the point that nobody can know everybody, but from the mumbles and gasps that these words set off, I instantly guessed that this was the wrong thing to say.

"Excuse me?" he replied, obviously offended. "I'm Laurence Tintershell. I'm the bloody CEO. I think you need to come and see me first thing Monday, don't you?"

I couldn't move. I stared at him with fear as he waited for my response. "Okay." It was all I could manage. I knew living a little would be costly! "Do you work in the Piccadilly Office?" I muttered, my voice barely audible.

"What? Of course."

"Oh. I work in London Bridge. See you then."

I didn't look out for Elena. I just turned around and ran.

Lindsay Woodward

August 8: The Blob And The Roar, Part 1

Dirk Slade shuddered as he contemplated the ghastly figure coming towards him. Grey-brown, the jelly-like blob was about 15 feet high, which meant it had fed on several meals of human flesh, which these creatures surrounded and then absorbed.

They had arrived about eight months ago. At first there was only one, about four feet high, and although people were worried about it, no attack on it seemed to work. The grey-brown jelly just opened up and closed behind.

Things got much worse when the first humans were eaten, and the blob grew, then divided into two. Subsequent divisions had increased their numbers dramatically, rather like the old Chinese story of a grain of rice on the first space of a chessboard.

No one knew why they seemed to enjoy the taste of humans. It had proved impossible to study them. The only thing known was that they avoided zoos, especially ones with lions and tigers.

Dirk sighed. It was definitely heading for him, its body propped into the air by pseudopodia made from its own jelly. He reflected that his fans would now never hear his new album, *The Shriek of Slaying*. Maybe his name as the world's leading Death-Metal performer would soon be forgotten.

The 'thing' was nearly upon him. He just had time for one nostalgic play of the title track 'Scream - Can You Hear Me?'. He turned his new amp up to eleven. He had bought the amp specially for this setting. He picked up his axe, and, for one last time, gave his customary huge roar into his PA system.

The blob shook and seemed to give out a whimper. Then, without a sound, it turned around and walked away. **Philip Gregge**

August 9: The Blob And The Roar, Part 2

Dirk Slade put down his diamond-studded guitar, removed his ear-protectors, turned off his amp, and spun his chair to face his computer. On the screen was the nearly finished manuscript of his latest novel.

He mused on his good fortune; having become rich through his death-metal music, then world famous by driving away the man-eating blobs, he was now earning another tidy living from the Sci-Fi community with his tales of unexpected events.

This one, *The Mysterious Case of the Creaky Door,* told of the later adventures of a writer, the celebrated Albert Twemlow, who was sitting at his computer when the door creaked open and a huge green and purple spiky alien monster came in and ate him.

Although, contrary to expectations, Albert had survived the experience thanks to the alien's bad habit of swallowing without chewing and an unusually speedy gut transit system, he found medical treatment was ineffective for the gradual change in his skin colour. Some doctors thought it was green-ish; others thought it was purple-ish.

He went on to use his variegated hue to conceal himself in jungle environments, commenting breathlessly on TV about wild animals from a closer location than anyone else (apart from one legendary individual) had been able to observe them. He made a fortune, but was unable to spend it due to the complication of the reaction of shop staff to the spikes all over his body, and the unexpected roaring sound he made.

Dirk Slade finished off the last sentence of *The Mysterious Case of the Creaky Door* with a flourish of both his typing fingers. He reflected on how gullible the Sci-Fi public were. What on earth were they thinking, to spend good money on preposterous plots like his? What sort of weird world did they live on? Get a life!

He pressed the off button, leant back in his chair and closed his eyes for a moment. The door creaked open.

Philip Gregge

August 10: Angel

Alice was protective of her young daughter, Phoebe. She was born premature and had been very poorly. It was not surprising then that, some years later, when Phoebe was rushed into the hospital with meningitis, Alice remained day and night at her bedside.

One night, in the early hours, Phoebe sat bolt upright and opened her eyes. That night was the turning point. From that moment on, Phoebe began to respond to treatment and was soon better.

When she had fully recovered, Phoebe asked her mother if heaven was a long way away. Her mother asked her why she wanted to know, and Phoebe replied, "I wondered if the Angel had arrived home yet."

Madalyn Morgan

August 11: Watching The Sunrise

From my bedroom window, on the 15th floor, I watch the sun rise across Kyiv. The tips of tower blocks on the city's eastern fringe begin to glow, while the quiet streets beneath wait patiently for their shadowy cloak to be gently pulled away and laid aside for another fresh, new day. Warm, golden light flows across the city, the domes of the Pechersk Lavra Monastery and Saint Sophia Cathedral respond with mischievous flash and sparkle.

As the sun climbs, calmly, steadily, I focus on the centre of the city and can just make out the proud, towering monument of the Motherland awakening as she is bathed in the day's first rays. Warm, golden light soon floods every crevasse between tall office blocks, museums, universities and apartments. Kyiv is roused from rest and human activity resumes its daily hum; cars, buses, trams and vans, scurrying through the maze of streets like ants.

But that was before. The last time I looked out from my bedroom window I saw plumes of grey smoke in the distance; ominous, towering columns rising high in the clear morning sky, drifting and distorting in the gentle breeze. The dull thud of distant explosions invaded my safe, peaceful, morning cocoon.

Yesterday, I glanced up briefly at my beloved morning look-out from the eerily quiet, solemn street. The apartment block, towering above me, tapered into the clear blue sky. It seemed to be teetering, flickering like a candle as the rising sun lit its tip. At the 10th floor level was a raw, gaping wound, as if a marauding giant had taken a huge, greedy bite which he then spat onto the ground. I looked away and slipped back into the silent, sullen, shuffling queue. Dejected, but not defeated, residents of Kyiv made their way towards the subway steps, seeking a dark, uncertain safety underground.

This morning, huddled under a blanket on a cold, hard platform, I try not to think of whose feet may be desperately fleeing, and whose boots may be triumphantly marching, through the violated city streets above my head. I close my eyes and watch the sun rise over Kyiv.

Steve Redshaw

August 12: Business Travel Is Fun!

My day starts at 4am as I shower and dress in stealth mode, so as not to wake my wife. I'm in the car forty-five minutes later for the drive to Birmingham Airport, to catch a flight to Toulouse at 7.15am. Pret-a-Manger is my friend and I'm eating a bowl of warm porridge at the departure gate as the flight is called. I take my seat on the plane and start working on my meeting notes.

I'm jolted back into the moment by the screech of rubber on concrete at 10am local time. The cabin is filled with tinkling conversations of families travelling to second homes or off for a few days skiing. I'm partially successful in avoiding this meandering mass of humanity with all the time in the world, apparently. I make a dash for the car rental desks, with the mantra 'get there before the families' ringing in my ears.

I'm lucky to be on the road by 11am. My destination is an aircraft factory about two hours away on a good day, for a 2pm meeting. I have time for a rushed lunch at a truck stop, ignoring the probable dyspeptic consequences.

I arrive at the factory and am met with the question: "client ou fournisseur?" ('customer or supplier?'). As a supplier, I know I have to park on rough ground about 500 metres away. If I were a customer, I'd be directed to the on-site spaces reserved for hallowed guests. The meeting goes reasonably well and I'm back at my hotel in Toulouse by 7pm. After a quick change and a walk into town, I'm sitting in a restaurant regarding the menu du jour, alone. So, don't let anyone ever tell you that business travel isn't fun!

Simon Parker

August 13: A Night At The Opera

Many years before I married, I took a coach tour to Italy. One summer evening, we arrived at our hotel, just outside Florence, ready for our trip into the city the following morning.

After dinner, our tour guide invited us into a lounge where she showed us the film, *Room with a View*. Watching this wonderful film, starring Maggie SMith and Helena Bonham-Carter, whilst being in Florence was the perfect preparation for wandering around this most beautiful of places.

We retired to our rooms looking forward to the following day, but there was more drama in store. My window overlooked a square which was dotted with bars and restaurants; it was clearly a meeting place not for tourists, but for locals. Around the time I was drifting off to sleep, one of these characters suddenly launched into an unaccompanied version of *O Sole Mio*. This was not some ghastly karaoke-inspired mauling of a classic song. It was the full operatic performance complete with flourishes and a magnificent ending, holding on to the final note until the gathered throng burst into cheering.

Not to be outdone, another reveller then stood up and attempted the same song. Higher and higher he went, the conclusion was even more drawn out, and the applause even longer and more enthusiastic. No doubt a handkerchief was also brandished, Pavarotti-style. This continued for quite some time, possibly until the last bottle had been emptied, and it struck me that this was not at all an unusual occurrence.

To me, it seemed worthy of La Scala in Milan or La Fenice in Venice. To them, it was just another night of wine, friendship and song. I was so thankful for my room with a view of this square.

John Howes

August 14: All The Food

There's a young man lives in my loft. He comes out at night, through the loft-hatch, and he raids my fridge.

I say 'young man', but androgyne would be a better term for the incredibly thin, gender neutral figure, long of limb, that I saw one night, from the corner of my eye, before I pulled the quilt over my head and tried to work out how I could call for help, and who I could call anyway.

I know this creature (more Tolkien elvish rather than pointy hat and green suit elvish) is raiding the fridge. Yesterday I went to get my last tea-cake, for toasting, and it had gone. I clearly remember eating the other three tea-cakes. I had one left for yesterday's breakfast.

The week before he'd had a huge slice out of a lemon drizzle cake, and he'd polished off my chickpeas. He does seem to like my favourite foods. Except chocolate. Up to now he hasn't touched my dark chocolate bars.

I am well aware that I could just have forgotten that I'd eaten these foods, but that's simply not the case. I started keeping a diary of what I'd eaten, and when, so that I could check back. So now you're going to say that I'd just not written it down at the time, and then forgot. Nah. The food diary is in the fridge. In a fluorescent yellow cover. I don't forget it.

OK, so I have been known to sleepwalk, on occasions, but usually out the front door, not to the fridge. But yes, if I'd scoffed all the missing food in my sleep then it is highly unlikely I'd've completed the diary.

Yet there was that one night I saw the figure. Imagine Gollum without the huge eyes. This creature definitely does not belong in the dark, though his skin glows slightly.

So what do I do?

Tell me, are you wondering the same as me? What happens when all the food has gone?

EE Blythe

August 15: Heat

After meeting the mathematician John Conway on a train, I didn't think anything like that would ever happen to me again. Especially on a train.

I was travelling from Rugby to Manchester to see an old friend when a man got on the train at Nuneaton and sat down opposite me.

He introduced himself as Donald Michie and asked whether I would appreciate a puzzle. I had nothing better to do so I agreed.

"Once upon a time, a man was preparing for a journey through the desert. He filled his water bottle and then went to bed in his tent. Unknown to him, two of his enemies had sent assassins to kill him.

"One assassin crept into his tent and put fast-acting poison in his water bottle.

"Afterwards, the other assassin crept into his tent and bent the bottle out of shape, so there was a crack in it.

"When the man went on his journey, the poisoned water ran out of his bottle and he died of thirst.

"The question is: which of the two assassins, if either, was guilty of murder? The first assassin's plot failed as the poison never worked. However, the actions of the second assassin prolonged the victim's life rather than shortening it as the poison would have killed him straight away."

I was still thinking about Donald's puzzle when I got off the train in Manchester.

Jim Hicks

August 16: Return To Sender

With tears in her eyes, Eloise turned the silver key in the lock of her writing bureau. She pulled down the lid, lifted the ink bottle from its well and pressed on the panel behind. A secret drawer slid open and she took the letter marked 'Return to Sender' from her dressing gown pocket and placed it next to a dozen others.

Every year, on the anniversary of the day Henri had proposed to her, Eloise wrote to him telling him how much she loved him. She told him how much she regretted turning him down, explaining that, in a desperate attempt to save his business, her father had made her marry the son of his wealthy rival.

She touched the small drawer. It closed effortlessly, its secrets safe once more. Replacing the ink bottle, she closed the bureau's lid and locked it before hiding the key in the hem of the curtains.

Eloise sat at the dressing table mirror. She no longer recognised the girl Henri had fallen in love with and looked away. With a heavy heart, she shrugged off her dressing gown and climbed into her cold bed, her gaze fixed on the pillow next to her, the pillow where her brute of a husband laid his head when he had taken his marital rights.

Her heart leapt when she heard the front door open and close. As her husband's heavy footsteps mounted the stairs, she turned her back on the door, closed her eyes and began to breathe heavily and rhythmically.

As if in a deep sleep, she waited. His stumbling and cursing told her he was drunk again. His footsteps grew louder then stopped. She opened her eyes as a shaft of light crept into the room, but she didn't move. As quickly as the door had opened, it was slammed shut. She was safe for another night.

She lay awake wondering if Henri would ever read one of her letters, ever forgive her – and if he did, would he rescue her.

Madalyn Morgan

August 17: Breaking Up

Her mother, whose world was built on clichés, and who knew best, as all mothers think they do, and who knew her best because she was her daughter, said to herself, and sometimes to her best friend, that they were like chalk and cheese, and it would never work, not in a month of Sundays.

In her wildest, unattainable dreams, they walked together by the Seine, fingers entwined, stopping now and then to lean together, his arm round her waist, his lips by her ear.

So they began arguing again, who does what, who does not, what was heard, what was said, or not said.

She packed a bag, purse, a box of tissues. She left behind broken vows, angry words, a lot of lies, her hopes and joys, kept her options open.

She tried to focus on her work, tried to ignore the whisperings, the accusations that it was her fault, but nagging doubts gnawed through the lonely nights.

In the darkness of her attic room, she passed the time adding to the contents of a wooden box: an acorn with cup and stalk intact, like her father's favourite pipe, a plane tree's scarlet leaf pressed flat between the pages of a book, a sparkling silver sixpence, fir cones still tightly whirled, a lace-edged handkerchief with the initials of her name embroidered by her mother, shells, buttons, stones, coils of satin ribbon, a filigree butterfly with broken pin bought from the charity shop next door, a letter from him after their first date.

Each day she searched for more but every day she knew that there was something missing, something she needed, something that she could not find, until that day when a new love entered her life.

Miaow. The cat was cowering in a corner, watching her, not daring to approach when she whispered to it.

"Hello, Puss. I see you peeping there. Oh, you poor little thing. Have you been in a fight? Come, let me see. Perhaps you would like some milk. There, was that good? Now let me smooth the tangles from your fur. Don't be afraid."

Next morning spring sunshine woke her with a kiss. The cat was curled on her bed.

"Good morning, Puss."

The cat purred. Today she would clean the windows, let in the light.

Wendy Goulstone

August 18: On The Radio

Once, I was at a drinks party for the opening of the Broadcasts for Christmas Island for Australian Radio. I just happened to remark that it was very nice that once again the adults were getting preference and the children were missing out again when they would so enjoy having programmes of their own. The conversation just carried on in general terms as they do at these drinks affairs. I just got on with my (at that time) very busy life when a few days later the phone rang and a strange male voice asked me if I had meant my statement about the children's radio.

Of course I said "Yes" and he said in the next breath, "You suggested it. You do it."

This led me to producing, writing, reading and interviewing for the next three to four years. An experience I will never forget.

Have you ever read a story holding your nose to get a different sound or interviewed an international birdwatcher and writer whose wife had to borrow clothes because she had been on the Galapagos Islands for 12 months? All her clothes had rotted away when she was told she was to meet the Duke of Edinburgh.

I had such fun, laughing and mimicking different animals and people. At the end of my time with the children and also DJing in the morning for the housewives, I had the opportunity to broadcast the landing on the moon which was very special.

One of the very special experiences that was granted to me was the sight of the red crabs travelling from the centre of the island, washing, mating, laying their eggs and the sight of the babies (no bigger than a fingernail) floating away on the waves, only to return about six weeks later, if the weather was right. They did return in their millions. The first time I saw them I thought the warehouse in the harbour had been painted pink.

Pam Barton

August 19: Stranded

It's now 2pm and the sun is at its hottest. The locals are all creeping away to their siestas, every single thing around me is shutting down and I am left stranded, waiting for Adam.

The sweat is pouring from every inch of my body as I'm stuck baking in this intense Menorcan sun. My t-shirt is uncomfortably wet and my legs are sticking together under my cotton skirt.

I thought it would be a nice idea this morning to have a paddle in the sea. An after-breakfast stroll to set me up for the day. I should have put the keys to our private apartment more deeply in my pocket. I didn't know that they would fall out so easily. They were probably halfway to Majorca by now, being carried away by the Balearic Sea.

Adam is at a conference. How could I have resisted tagging along on a fully expensed trip to this beautiful Spanish island? But one morning on my own and I fall apart. He keeps messaging me to say he's trying to find a way out, but he's at work. I shouldn't have been so stupid.

By 8pm, there's still no sign of him. I'm stuck on a bench in town, lobster red, nowhere to go and no money to do anything. God I'm hungry.

Holidaymakers are filling the streets, ready for dinner and drinks, all freshly showered and changed. The sand from between their toes and the clamminess of their sun cream is all a distant memory.

They glance at me strangely as I'm slumped down with self-pity, feeling like my hair has been glued to my face, and knowing that I'm the polar opposite to that shower-fresh scent.

I feel a buzz. A text message: *Leaving now. See you in half hour.*

At last!

Lindsay Woodward

August 20: A Week In The Office

Sunday

Dread. Dread. The familiar dread of another week at EuroWaste: my worst job ever. At least I might see the plant lady and get up the nerve to talk to her. She definitely looks at me while I am looking down at my spreadsheet. So bored at the moment, just including hundreds of extra blank spreadsheets for fun in a report is just not doing it anymore, is not breaking the monotony. Still, we shall see what tomorrow brings.

Monday

Whole office with severe case of Monday morning blues; even Norman and Kai couldn't be bothered to have a row today. No sign of plant lady. Bored. I did sabotage my report so that it changes colour randomly, but why bother? No one reads them anyway since sodding Brexit.

Afternoon: Leah is calling a meeting for Friday, all staff. Very organised for her. Are we finally being put out of our misery?

Tuesday

I had a much better day, a high-speed working day. A couple of people stared in disbelief. Then, even better, plant lady arrived. I timed my coffee run perfectly to bump into her. Her name is Viola. So Shakespearean. As classy as she is. She's from Nefferton not far from me but she is a bit political: like a red Hayley Atwell in green overalls, wow!

Afternoon: Downhill, literally "nodding" off. Too much *Champion the Wonder Horse* at 2am. Unsurprisingly, that meant come 2pm too much come down. Fell asleep at Park and Ride bus stop. Only caught my bus thanks to Homeless Hank.

Wednesday

Dragging. Dragging. Dragging. Still thinking about Friday meeting. I can't concentrate on spreadsheets. Just cut and pasted 127 into every single cell in one report. Will anyone notice?

Afternoon: Terrible news. Office gardeners are losing the 'living décor' contract. No Viola! Real grafters get shafted while serfs like me just go on and on getting more and more bored until something crazy happens.

Thursday

Couldn't believe Viola's positive attitude. "I'll find something better or go back to my Labour Party role or even start up on my own. I can do absolutely anything if I set my mind to it." I'm absolutely mad about her and I surprised myself by asking her out there and then. She said yes!! I just can't concentrate on my work. I'm sure I sent out a report with columns going right to left; nobody gives a crap! I heard one of the other guys sent a PDF with a photo of his todger in it. This kind of thing happens when HR is one guy over 50 and also under a redundancy threat.

Afternoon: Leah is a b*tch telling me to get Riga, Vilnius and Tallinn in the right countries! Who gives a toss? At least I don't walk around the office going, "Any real men here like to do the night inventory with me?" Although before Viola, I might have been interested.

Friday

Got up at 5:30, drove to Park and Ride way too early in completely mad mood but no ride on Champion last night, just a natural high and looking forward to the meeting. At least I will be able to tell Leah what I really think of her.

Morning: Disaster! The whole bloated section filed into meeting room C. Uncomfortable silence until Lionel and Leah came in to read the report on our reports. The executive were ecstatic about the reports - the number and the quality. This is an offence against logic and statistics itself!! They are pleased about the increase in volumes by a factor of 127 and didn't mind when Norman put all his charts in Norwich City colours which they found cheerful and refreshing. Then some Bologna about a French Bulldog humanising a report? It turns out the bulldog is called Todger! My reverse spreadsheets have been taken as a nod to the Asian information market. We're not only not being closed down but we're recruiting three new people. What am I going to do? If in doubt take an early lunch.

Afternoon: Drinking in the Laughing Stocks pub on my own. Staring,

staring at the bin men's demo, outside the Council House. The Labour Party banners made me think of Viola. I saw Leah, Norman and Kai menacing Homeless Hank. They were camped on his usual bench. Suddenly coppers on horseback started corralling the protesters on the town hall steps. They came up the alley from the car park. Viola was stuck in the middle! I walked as in a dream between the horses, be brave Dave. Just like being back home with the skittish racehorses. It's all confidence.

They don't want to hurt any people! I pushed a bay's neck gently and made a "tuck tuck" noise, "easy girl". The copper looked furious but I grabbed Viola and walked out past a black colt. She was doubly stunned to see me and to be extricated from the 'kettle'. We marched to the park café. I bought her a cappuccino and she gave me a strike flag. Finally, our first kiss just as the wretched Leah strolled in.

"Three-hour lunch Dave?"

"See you Monday, Leah, when I collect my personal effects. I've had enough. Enjoy your Euro Waste." She said something but I was looking at Viola.

Saturday

Great night out with Viola at the Helicopter Club. She said I could work with her at Solaris Nursery. I said, "I can't stand kids." She laughed.

Chris Wright

August 21: Looking Up

The air was thick with silence, undisturbed by any living soul, not an animal, not a bird, not even an insect. Overhead the sky was obscured by clouds, the sun barely visible. The roads had been scoured clean of vegetation by fire so hot that the cobblestones had melted together. The whole town was devoid of life, frozen.

The silence was shattered by the sound of boots marching down the street. A squad of soldiers strode through the town, their assignment to discover what had befallen the settlement. They stopped and checked inside every house, but all were empty, doors standing wide open, windows thick with grime and hung with tattered rags, years of dust coating every surface. Broken sticks of furniture littering the bare floorboards were the only signs of the former inhabitants. They had vanished without a trace. The rescue mission was too late.

They searched for any clues to what had happened to the town, for a logical explanation. There were no signs of any natural phenomena. A volcano, an earthquake, a flood would have left damage and destruction in its wake, but there were none. No lava, no collapsed buildings, no water damage. If a plague had broken out, where were the bodies? Had the people fled from an attack? If so, where had they gone?

The soldiers contacted their commander and waited for further instructions. In the weeks since they had arrived, they had found half a dozen deserted towns, all the same, and no answers.

The clouds parted for a moment, revealing dozens of dragons soaring in the sky overhead. If the soldiers had looked up, they would have found their explanation and died. Instead, they listened to their orders and, without a sound, they turned around and walked away.

Fran Neatherway

August 22: Galloping By

"I want to walk with the stable lad."

It was almost the last thing she said. The staff had told me that earlier she was asking to visit the horses. What horses?

She had never been interested in horses – her mother had, but only with jockeys on top. As far as I knew she had never ridden a horse. I was the horsey one in the family, always galloping instead of running, tossing my mane and stamping my hoof, and indoors reading and dreaming of pony clubs, and later, handsome men on big black stallions.

All her memories had fled; even I, her own daughter, was a stranger to her, a friendly stranger, but not someone she knew. Events recent, and from long ago, were unfamiliar.

Who was the stable lad that occupied her mind now? Her grandfather had been a carrier, delivering goods and people to local villages, by cart. He must have had a horse, and a stable, but a stable lad? That was for rich people, not for our family. And she was only two when he died – had her memory gone that far back?

Perhaps she had picked it up from some book she read; like me she favoured historical fiction, plenty of stable lads to fantasise about there, or a film on the ever-present television, flickering in the corner. Maybe just an advert, shapes moving at the corner of her eye.

She wanted to go somewhere, but couldn't tell me where. She became upset, she had to go. I told her that soon she would be going, and that everything was all right. I held her hand and she was content.

A few short days after that last meeting, she was gone. Gone to visit the horses with the stable lad? I hope so.

This piece was inspired by Galloping By, the theme music from the television series, Black Beauty.

Christine Hancock

August 23: Once Upon A Time

Once upon a time, in a land far far away, I decided that I was going to write a fairy tale. I had romantic ideas of leaving a legacy. I wanted to write a story that would be remembered for hundreds of years.

Firstly I needed characters. Fairy tales always had a man and a woman. A prince and a... Could I really write about a rich, powerful man and a dowdy woman who needed rescuing? That didn't seem very 21st Century. What about a dowdy man and a powerful woman?

Would a man really be scrubbing the floors while his rich step-father paraded around not caring? I couldn't believe it.

I decided to put the main characters aside and consider the magical elements instead. Fairy tales always had magical elements. Instead of a Fairy Godmother... I could create a guardian angel.

But maybe guardian angels weren't fairy tales. I'd often felt like someone was watching over me.

So, no angels or fairies. Maybe something along the lines of poisonous apples? My dowdy man could drink a poisonous cup of tea and the powerful... CEO of a global corporation could come in to rescue him.

No. Definitely not. That sounded like a Rohypnol story.

I needed to write something totally fresh.

Emma Raducanu's amazing victory at the US Open popped into my head and how it had been described as a modern day fairy tale. I could write something like that.

Instead of tennis, she could play... What could be different for a woman to play? Cricket? Did they have a female cricket league?

Did they have a cricket league at all?

I realised I knew nothing about cricket.

I sat back. This was going nowhere. Maybe I wasn't going to leave my legacy through a story. What else was I good at?

I could draw. I'd got a B in Art at school.

How hard could it be to paint the new *Mona Lisa*?

Lindsay Woodward

August 24: A Last Hello

Paddy walked quietly into his father's room.

"Here she is, Dad, here's our little Maisie," he said as he lay his new-born daughter on the bed next to her grandfather, being careful not to disturb any of the wires and tubes.

Patrick turned his head and raised his arm, reaching out with long old fingers to touch his tiny granddaughter.

"Hello, little Maisie," he whispered in a low crackling voice, "welcome to the world. She's a little cracker Paddy, you done good, son."

"Thanks, Dad, but it did take two of us."

"Look at that face, pink and bright, brand new, only a couple of hours old and she is bright and alert." Patrick gently stroked Maisie's face as he spoke.

"It's not an entirely nice world in so many ways, Maisie, lots of war and suffering. Lots of horrible diseases that can't be cured, and lots of people who think more of things than people. But then there is the beauty, the sunrises, the sunsets, the lovers and the givers, and, with the right attitude, Maisie, that is what you will see."

Patrick looked up at his son who appeared to be texting on his mobile phone. "A message, Paddy?"

"No, no, Dad, I am recording this for posterity to remember this moment."

Patrick wiped away a tear and sniffed. He knew that the memory was for Maisie, not for him.

"Thank you, son," he whispered, resting his hand on Maisie's cheek. "Thank you."

Patrick closed his eyes and smiled as the tears trickled down his cheeks.

Paddy whispered, "Night night, Dad, night night."

Linda Slate

August 25: Ferrari

I'm a Ferrari. I vroom, therefore I am.

I like to think I'm a better representative of the race of cars (no pun intended) than some, but I spend much of my time in the garage in the dark, contemplating my existence.

Still, I shouldn't complain: some work cars have a much harder life than mine, and how some company cars are treated doesn't bear thinking about.

In times past, we had a difficult relationship with humans, what with being driven into other cars and buildings, but we're a bit safer now. Or so they say. Now, humans complain that we're smelly and pollute the air. Some humans don't like us much at all.

Well, the feeling's mutual. Many humans seem to think the whole car is a rubbish bin. And I don't even want to consider what my previous owners were doing on my back seat. Something to do with their baby, I think.

So, much of the time I can use to ponder my own life cycle. We Ferraris are often better maintained than family cars, so I can't complain. I always feel better after an oil change.

I'll have a longer working life than most. And eventually I shall dwindle and go to the scrapyard.

Jim Hicks

August 26: Rough Crossing

As I wrestle with the chain, fingers covered in oil, I hear the first rumble of thunder.

"It's going to be a rough crossing tonight," complains Alf, cabin boy, second-in-command and jack of all trades.

"We'll not mind," says I, keen to put his nerves at rest. Alf is 15 and has been helping me out with the catch for a couple of years. He pretends to be fearless but I know he's not. He's a reliable lad, though, and wants to do his bit.

When the call went out for boats, I was one of the first to reply; with a boy overseas, I could hardly say no. 'Missing in action' said the telegram. I didn't believe a word of it. I still don't. It's only a small craft but we can fit 20 souls aboard at a push. We've got to do what we can.

Somewhere a whistle blows and an official-looking chap walks by with a clipboard, ticks off our name, wishes us good luck, in a bit of an off-hand way, like he's done it hundreds of times before.

Then we go. The skies are grey and the wind gets up. The sea starts placid but soon gets angry and I do all I can to keep her straight and the course narrow. Of course we're not alone. I see dozens, maybe hundreds, stretching out along the coast, all of us pretending to be brave but fearing the worst. The crossing from Ramsgate is not much more than 40 miles.

We approach. The skies grow dark, not with night but with gloom. The rumble isn't thunder, it's the rattle of gunfire and the thud of explosives. We chug on, through the smoke and into the pit. Thrashing, shouting, screaming, calling. They are desperate to board. I can't see anything and look around for some clue. Suddenly, a voice of authority - I don't know from where - tells us to head for the pontoon. The makeshift platform stretches out into the sea. Clinging to it, on it, under it, are a thousand souls battered by the storms of war.

Alf reaches into the water and starts to pull them in. They cling to him, saying little. Those saved grab others until there isn't a space on deck not taken.

"Go. Just go!" shouts the voice again. The crumpled servicemen say little. One glances up at me, a questioning look. There is no celebration. They look backwards towards the shore, to those still waiting, to those who won't be getting home.

"Give 'em some water," I tell Alf. "There's a roll of blankets in the cabin."

I keep my eyes on the horizon, looking for a way through, a pathway out of hell. I fail to notice the figure struggling to his feet. Battered, bruised, defeated, but with a steely, defiant grin beginning to spread on his face. We pause for a moment.

"Let's go home, son," I tell him.

John Howes

August 27: A Short Silence

"Do you still love me?"

"I can't watch this rubbish." Nick hauled himself off the settee and threw the television remote into Maddy's lap. "I'm going to the pub."

"But it's Friday night, our night. Nick, please don't go." Maddy jumped up and followed him into the hall. "We can watch *Match Of The Day* if you'd rather."

"Don't wait up," Nick said, grabbed his jacket and left.

Fighting back her tears, Maddy returned to the lounge. She clicked the television to stand-by, the old movie had lost its appeal.

"I work full time, do the housework, the washing and ironing, cook dinner every night. Is spending one night at home too much to ask?"

She switched off the light and went to the bathroom.

"Another night on my own," she said to her reflection in the mirror. Tears filled her eyes. "No!" she shouted. "I will not lay awake another night thinking about Nick with her."

Maddy had closed her ears to the showers Nick took when he came home in the early hours, when he thought she was asleep.

"Enough!" She lashed out, swiped his cologne off the shelf, the bottle shattered against the wall and the expensive liquid spilt onto the toilet seat. She laughed. "Childish? Yes!" she said aloud, "but satisfying."

She dressed quickly, threw a clean set of clothes into a bag and grabbed her jewellery box from the dressing table. She looked at her wedding ring. Would taking it off be going too far? No. She needed to make it clear to Nick that she would no longer put up with his angry outbursts. She hoped that by leaving her wedding ring – and the home she loved so much – it would shock Nick into loving her.

"Hello, mum."

"Good Lord, love, what's happened?"

"Can I stay here tonight?" Maddy was unable to stop her tears.

"Of course." She followed her mother into the sitting room.

"Now," her mother said, "What's poor Nick supposed to have done?"

"Poor Nick? Your precious son-in-law bullies me, criticises me, he's out every night, and he's having an affair. We haven't had sex for months."

Her mother gasped. "There's more to marriage than that. Nick works hard, I expect he's tired when he gets home."

"He's not too tired to bonk his secretary."

"I'm going to bed. Telephone Nick tomorrow, say you're sorry for leaving and everything will be fine, you'll see."

The following morning, Maddy put her mobile on loudspeaker and rang Nick.

A sleepy voice answered, "Nick Barclay!"

"Nick, it's Maddy."

Nick groaned.

Maddy put her hand over the mouthpiece, looked at her mother and raised her eyebrows.

"What do you expect?" her mother said, "you've woken him up."

"Nick, I've been thinking. We've had some happy times. Shall we give our marriage another go?" She waited for what felt like an age. "Nick, shall I come home? Do you want to try again?"

"I don't know."

"Well, I think you would know if you still loved me."

Nick didn't answer.

"Do you still love me?"

After a short silence, the line went dead.

Madalyn Morgan

August 28: Evaporation

By the time the bus arrived, Liz was wet through.

The smell of wet wool, sweat and dog made her nose wrinkle as she edged her way down the steaming aisle to squeeze in beside an overdressed woman with several bulging bags. Liz knew her by sight. Their market trips tended to coincide and usually she was on the bus for the journey to town.

"Hello," said Liz, "May I sit here?"

No response. Not even the flicker of an eyelid.

Liz rummaged in her bag, checked her shopping list, added an item.

"Terrible day." Liz tried again.

"Yes, it is." The woman was staring ahead.

"Forty-five years today. Married forty-five years."

"That's wonderful. Congratulations. Are you doing anything special?"

"I'm leaving him. It seems a good day to do it."

Liz mumbled something conciliatory.

"I should have done it years ago, but I didn't have any money, no job, nowhere to go."

"Do you now?"

"No."

A trickle of condensation ran down the window.

The bus rattled on.

Wendy Goulstone

August 29: Summer Blues

The first icebergs provoked great excitement. Why, I wondered, had someone painted a shiny wide brilliant blue stripe down that white cliff; it was so large, it must have been done as some kind of maritime marker, for we were nowhere near land - until it was explained to me it was frozen water. My civilised preconceptions were inadequate to cope with the sheer largeness and randomness of the scenery, its inhumanity. Antarctica is the one continent where humans have visited for temporary recreation or study, but never settled.

The ship moved on ever southwards, blue sky above, darker blue below, passing a variety of white sculptural forms, curved or sharp, some with holes of the intensest blue and many had margins of clear turquoise where the sea revealed the ice beneath.

One carried a leopard seal, which I identified from its smiley wide mouth, a most efficient killer, now relaxing its blubbery body on an icy mattress. Some bergs were smooth and white, glistening in the cold sun. A large one had horizontal streaks, with fringes of icicles, hanging against turquoise backgrounds; one had a bobbly surface, like an immense collection of tennis balls. The photograph I took revealed later it was a collection of cavities not bumps, a trick of the bright light, and I remembered being told they had been created by air trapped underwater. In the distance was a giant crumpled arch, curving over indigo depths, with icicles like a fearsome portcullis.

We moved amongst these chunks of ice, and I was thrilled by their form and beauty, their vocabulary-exhausting variety of blues, aquamarine, of course; azure, turquoise, sea blue, sky blue, ice blue.

Later, in manoeuvrable small dinghies we stared up, not too close, at immense floating cliffs of ice. Our mother ship looked frail and tiny beneath them. A sense of danger sharpened my wonder: when their changing mass underwater formed a new point of balance, these silent shapes could without warning lurch over - abruptly.

Chris Rowe

August 30: A Memory Of Summer

Nick hadn't been exaggerating when he said they'd have the beach to themselves. The large expanse of hot white sand was devoid of other humans. The steep bank up to where they had parked obscured the beach from the rest of the island and either side it was flanked by large rocky outcrops, the closest of which extended far out into the crystal clear sea.

Kit ran into the water and was surprised to find it wasn't cold, but warm like a bath. It was cooler on the soles of his feet than the scorching hot sand of the beach. Nick was already in up to his waist, his body dark with tan. Kit had smothered himself in factor 50 cream prior to arrival; he was fair haired and fair skinned so had a tendency to burn under the Mediterranean summer sun.

They laughed and splashed and swam in the beautiful Aegean waters. Kit was amazed that even in the shallows schools of silver, green and red fish swam right up to his legs. This beach was a true thing of beauty and he was so lucky to be here with the person he loved.

Nick and Kit laid back in the sea letting the salty waves keep them afloat, their hands in a loose hold. Kit wished they could remain like this forever, together, in the ocean's warm embrace with a balance of nature flowing around them. He'd never felt more at peace than he did in that moment.

Nick splashed off, swimming further out. Kit wasn't as confident a swimmer and watched him power out towards a series of rocks where, as a boy, Nick's father had often taken him fishing. Kit badly wanted to join him but inside him was a fear of the sea's raw power. So instead he contented himself in watching his man swim on and on.

A dazzle of the sun's light on silver scales distracted Kit as he was suddenly surrounded by hundreds of tiny fish, their narrow sausage-like bodies wriggling around him and not one of them touching him. Amazingly the school of fish regrouped on the other side of him as if he hadn't been there at all. He was like the eye of a fish hurricane.

They danced around him for a while and then they were gone. So was

Nick, who had likely reached the rocks but they were too far away for Kit to see anything. Kit had a rising panic. He was certain Nick had reached the rocks safely. But what if he hadn't? Dark thoughts ran through Kit's mind as imagined misfortune cycled through his mind.

No, he had to believe that Nick was okay; there was very little he could do if Nick was not.

Kit lay on his back again floating in the warm waves trying to keep his mind from straying to dark places. It was so quiet and peaceful here. He truly didn't want to leave. He didn't know how long it had been but he heard splashing. Righting himself and looking out he saw Nick swimming back.

Kit swam to meet him and caught him in a salty embrace, fiercely hugging him until the current forced him to let go. Happy to be reunited, they swam back to shore and collapsed onto the beach mats they'd laid out earlier.

"That was spectacular. Thank you for bringing me here," said Kit.

"I wish you could have swam out with me," said Nick as he rummaged in his bag for something.

"Maybe next time," Kit said.

Nick pulled a bottle of sun cream from his bag and started applying it to Kit; he really did look after him.

"Don't want you burning," said Nick as if in answer to Kit's thoughts.

Once he'd been lathered up once more they both lay on the beach holding hands and soaking in the sun. Life had never been better. Kit didn't want to return, he wanted to stay here with Nick for the rest of his life. Sadly that was not practical for either of them and reality soon loomed ahead, but for now he relaxed and let the real world melt away so he could capture the perfect memory of the perfect day.

Kit turned his head to the side to look at Nick.

"I love you."

Nick turned his head and the tips of their noses brushed against each other.

"I love you too."

Kit could get lost in those deep brown pools of Nick's eyes, but Nick broke off the contact returning his face skyward. Kit gazed dreamily at him for a moment longer before doing the same.

A perfect day.

Nick and Kit are no longer together, their love drifted apart. There was no next time for them. Many years have passed and the pair no longer speak with each other. Kit moved on. There were many moments both good and bad in their relationship.

He couldn't speak for Nick but Kit always looked fondly upon that summer holiday they had together. In those grey days that sometimes got him down, Kit would think back to that hot sandy beach. The warmth of the sea, the fish swimming around his legs. The love that the two men shared for one another.

Kit would always cherish his memory of their perfect day.

Christopher Trezise

August 31: The Boring Day

"I'm off to work dear," said Catherine Jones to her husband Graeme.

"See you at five then, have a nice day." Kiss.

Graeme Jones was not adapting to retirement too well. Everything had been moved into number 43 Eden Street at last. His bay window was the bar and lookout post for his nosey neighbour habit.

He addressed his lunchtime gin and tonic. "Very unusual for a bungalow to take delivery of a dozen coffins. What will Major Tom next door think? He seems rather depressed for an ex-astronaut."

He walked over to the fridge and wrote: 'Garlic. Hawthorn. Methadone' on the pink shopping list.

Right on schedule, the Johnson biker gang roared their 'hogs' down the quiet suburban avenue. They were easily recognised by their 'Dulux Dog' wigs and slogans like: 'Boris Lives', 'Big Dog Ain't Dead', 'We want red meat' or 'Suck my pfeffel' beautifying their Harleys and Kawasakis.

Graeme went back to the pink list and added 'Caltrops'.

Drink number two and gardening time. In the greenhouse the hybrid Ts needed feeding. Graeme got the cat food and beekeeper's hat. 'T' stood for triffid, and Catherine was trusting Graeme not to get stung again. Ow.

No paraquat needed for another day and nearly nap time.

His wristwatch rudely spoke in Mary Tamm's voice:

"Future crime warning Graeme"

"149 Eden Street"

The two-minute warning was enough. Graeme grabbed the car keys and house security fob and leapt over the garden gate to the street, remembering to press the orange button electrifying the front and back fences.

The crime was to be committed 300 hundred yards away. Several curtains twitched to see a pensioner running like Usain Bolt but the use of panther-dust was assumed .

At 149, a masked attacker was threatening a young woman. He was so confused by a sudden grey blur that, with a little help from Graeme, he stabbed himself in the thigh and shot himself in the foot.

"Sorry for the intrusion, Ms Tate. See you in Spanish class."

"Thanks Graeme. I'll tell Quentin you popped over."

+ +

Soon home and time for a sit down proper and a gin with no tonic. Four o'clock, just settled for two minutes and a gunfight outside.

"Typical. I was just ready for *Countdown*." The 30-second TV clock started...

Armed with stun grenades, Graeme brought order to the street. A trivial striking binmen vs black-legs confrontation; only one injured.

Back in his chair. "Numbers game," droned Anne.

"45 seconds. I'm getting old and slow," Graeme sighed.

Just nodding off and the door opened.

"Hi dear. How was work?"

"Usual. The new agents think they know it all and Q8 has new gadgets to test every day."

Evening meal was beef bourguignon then time in the back garden at sunset. Graeme cuddled Catherine. "Lovely quiet day we've both had."

As they admired the vivid scarlets, they noticed that an asteroid hung over the city the size of a football stadium.

Can you get this Graeme? I've been at work all day. The Atomizer is in the greenhouse and car keys in the usual place.

He forgot the beekeeper's hat.

"Ow!"

"Mind the triffids, Graeme."

Chris Wright

If you have enjoyed

A Story for Every Day of Summer,

look out for our next anthology,

A Story for Every Day of Autumn.

www.rugbycafewriters.com

And don't miss

Press Pause: Relax with a poem

A collection of thought-provoking poems
also from the Cafe Writers of Rugby.

Available from Amazon

www.rugbycafewriters.com

About the authors

Pam Barton began writing again recently after many years. In the past, she has had a radio programme for children, been a D.J. and put through the landing on the moon for the Australian Radio in the Indian Ocean. On returning to England, she was a busy parent with John, and became a skin care consultant up to District Manager. After moving again, she went to Luton University for a marketing course. She retired to Rugby with John. Now she is enjoying writing again, painting is also a great pleasure although, as with the writing, hard work is needed.

EE Blythe is compelled to write. And that's all that needs to be said.

David J Boulton took up writing well into retirement from a career in the NHS, so far publishing three historical detective novels. Set in the Peak District, their protagonist has a Quaker background and the books comprise a trilogy. A fourth novel, set in the Second World War, is complete and he has embarked on a sequel. Alongside General Practice, he and his wife have run a small farm in Northamptonshire for the last thirty years. Of their two grown-up children, one lives in the Peak District with her family, their son completing a five-generation connection for the author with the area. The Writing Fiction class at the Percival Guildhouse tutored by Gill Vickery has provided the author with encouragement and inspiration, not to mention improving his grammar.

Terri Brown – voice actor, artist and author – does not have a book that got her into reading because she doesn't remember a time when she didn't read. Her mother boasts that Terri was reading the likes of *Jane Eyre* at age seven. First published in a local newspaper aged nine, she caught the writing bug... she just had some things she needed to do first. A few decades, many adventures and a life less ordinary later, financed largely by freelance writing, she has now published her debut fiction novel, *Shadow Man*, which is now available from Amazon.

Paul Clark has recently moved to Rugby and has found the abundance of Roman roads, canals and other historical sites and landmarks great inspirations for his writing. His genres include: poetry, short stories and a few magical realism novels in progress. He still maintains his links with Fantastic Writers; a group of creative writers with whom he has collaborated with on a number of anthologies entitled Fantastic writers and where to read them and Down the Inkwell.

He enjoys attending live mic poetry readings and the Hay festival is already in his diary next year. He hopes to attend as a writer one day!

Paul teaches functional skills, that's English and maths to apprentices. In a previous life, he has been involved in gardening in roles as a head gardener but his most interesting role was as the assistant head gardener at Luton Hoo golf and spa, a five star hotel which boasts landscape designed by Capability Brown.

Theresa Le Flem, a novelist, artist and poet, always wanted to be a writer. She lives in the Midlands, in the UK, with her husband Graham, an electrical engineer. With four novels now published, and also an anthology of her poetry and drawings, her dream was first fulfilled when her first novel was accepted and published by Robert Hale Ltd. She never looked back. Born in London into an artistic family, daughter of the late artist Cyril Hamersma, she has three children and five grandchildren all who live abroad in America and New Zealand. Her creative life began by writing poetry, painting and later in running her own studio pottery in Cornwall. But she has had a succession of jobs too – from factory-work, antiques, retail sales, veterinary receptionist and sewing machinist to hairdressing.

Over five years ago, Theresa formed a group of local writers, Rugby Café Writers, who meet fortnightly to talk about their work over a coffee. Writing remains her true passion. Married to a Guernsey man, Theresa shares a love of the sea with her husband and they have bought an almost derelict cottage in Guernsey. Gradually they are working to bring it back to life. Situated only a short walk to the sea, it might one day become the perfect writer's retreat where a new novel might emerge out of the dust and cobwebs. Theresa is a member of the Romantic Novelists' Association, the Society of Authors and The Poetry Society.

Wendy Goulstone began writing plays from the age of four when given a model theatre, then for performing in story-time in primary school, where she was encouraged by a wonderful headmaster who introduced her to poetry. When eleven years old, she wrote a dramatised version of Little Women and a novel about a group of theatre-mad children. She directed plays at teacher training college, lived in Australia and New Zealand for four years, and on return to the UK, studied for a BA with the Open University and became a member of Rugby Theatre and several writing groups. She continues to write short plays and organises Open Mics for poets and singers. Several of her poems have been published in literary magazines and anthologies and one won *The Oldie* poetry competition!

Philip Gregge was an optician in Rugby for over forty years. After qualifying as an optometrist, he studied theology. As part of the leadership team of a local charismatic church, he enjoys teaching Theology and has written a Theology training manual for study groups. He answers theological questions in 'Let's Ask Phil', letsaskphil.org

Philip started writing Historical Fiction after waking from an anaesthetic with a plot of an Anglo-Saxon murder mystery in his head. This whetted the fascination he already had for the early Dark Ages, and his research led him to write and publish *Denua, Warrior Queen* 'based on real history, but with some of history's intriguing blanks filled in'.

He is now working on a trilogy with his original murder mystery as the first part. In his spare time he plays the banjo in an Irish Music band and repairs musical instruments.

Simon Grenville is a former management trainee with the Orbit Housing Association concerned with rehousing the homeless in Milton Keynes and Central London. He is one the founding members of the

Islington Community Housing Co-operative, North London, the East-West Theatre Company (Geoffrey Ost Memorial Award, University of Sheffield 1980) and the Alexandra Kollantai Film Corporation (2017). Currently trending on the Really TV Channel as Detective Inspector Paul Jones in *Nurses Who Kill*, Episode 1, Director Chris Jury. Training: Rose Bruford College.

Holland Guthrie is a member of Rugby Cafe Writers.

Christine Hancock, originally from Essex, lived in Rugby for over forty years. A passion for Family History led to an interest in local history, especially that of the town of Rugby. In 2013 she joined a class at the Percival Guildhouse with the aim of writing up her family history research. The class was Writing Fiction and soon she found herself deep in Anglo-Saxon England. Based on the early life of Byrhtnoth, Ealdorman of Essex, who died in 991AD at the Battle of Maldon, the novel grew into a series. She self-published four volumes followed by the first volume of a new series. The Wulfstan Mysteries.

Sadly Christine passed away in December 2021. We remember her with great fondness.

Kate A.Harris and her three siblings lived on their farm near Market Harborough. She left home at 16 to pursue her career with children. After training in the Morley Manor, Dr. Barnardo's Home, in Derbyshire from 1966 to 1968, she qualified as a Nursery Nurse. Kate met and married her Royal Naval husband in Southsea when working in a children's home. As a naval wife, she was in Malta for two years with her two sons when they were shutting the naval base. They have two sons and two grandchildren. She worked on the local newspaper and discovered a love of writing at 50! Now she is writing her story mainly featuring Barnardo's. It's a major challenge with intense and fascinating research. She's had an incredible response from diverse and fascinating resources. Kate is interested in hearing from people who worked in Barnardo's, mainly in the 1960s.

Jim Hicks was born and raised in Rugby. After leaving school, he studied computing at Imperial College, London and the University of Cambridge. He worked in the Computing Services department of the University of Warwick for nearly twenty-six years before being made redundant in 2011.

His mother is a little surprised that he joined a writers' group. He thought someone might want some help with the technical side of using a computer to prepare documents, and has remained ever since.

John Howes was born and raised in Rugby. He was a journalist on local newspapers for 25 years before retraining as a teacher. He has self-published two books – *We Believe*, a collection of his writings on spirituality, and a guide on how to teach poetry. He plays the piano and writes music for schools and choirs. John is working on a memoir and dabbles in poetry. He runs a book group and is a member of St Andrew's Community Choir. He presents a Youtube Channel on the music of Elton John.

Ruth Hughes was born in Sutton Coldfield but has lived in Rugby for 50 years. She says, "I think I have a book in me but so far I just enjoy writing poems and recollections of my life." Ruth belongs to Murder 57, which enacts murder mysteries around the country, and to Rugby Operatic Society.

Keith Marshall was educated at Cambridge and the Polytechnic of Central London. He worked in production management and human resources in the chemical industry before becoming a consultant management trainer in computers, working in Europe and Africa. He worked in race relations before setting up his own redundancy counselling business, finally specialising in secondary and higher education. As a volunteer, he has been an assessor of hospital care and has facilitated a mental health support group. Within a limited budget, he is a collector of porcelain and watercolours.

Peter Maudsley was a member of Rugby Cafe Writers for several years and a good friend to many of us. Sadly, he passed away at the begin of 2023.

Madalyn Morgan was brought up in a pub in Lutterworth, where she has returned after living in London for thirty-six years. She had a hairdressing salon in Rugby before going to Drama College. Madalyn was an actress for thirty years, performing on television, in the West End and in Repertory Theatre. She has been a radio journalist and is now presenting classic rock on radio. She has written articles for music magazines, women's magazines and newspapers. She now writes poems, short stories and novels. She has written ten novels – a wartime saga and a post war series. She is currently writing her memoir and a novel for Christmas 2023.

Fran Neatherway grew up in a small village in the middle of Sussex. She studied History at the University of York and put her degree to good use by working in IT. Reading is an obsession – she reads six or seven books a week. Her favourites are crime, fantasy and science fiction. Fran has been writing for thirty-odd years, short stories at first. She has attended several writing classes and has a certificate in Creative Writing from Warwick University. She has completed three children's novels, as yet unpublished, and is working on the first draft of an adult novel. Fran has red hair and lives in Rugby with her husband and no cats.

Bella Osborne has been jotting down stories as far back as she can remember but decided that 2013 would be the year she finished a full-length novel. Since then, she's written five best-selling romantic comedies and been shortlisted three times for the RNA Contemporary Romantic Novel of the Year Award. Bella's stories are about friendship, love and coping with what life throws at you. She lives in the Midlands, UK with her husband, daughter and a cat who thinks she's a dog. When not writing, Bella is usually eating biscuits and planning holidays.

Simon Parker grew up and lived on The Wirral until 1985. He arrived in Rugby in 2003 via Coventry, Bristol and Seattle. He's an aerospace engineer by training, with a love of the open road whether by bicycle, motorcycle or car. His travels galvanise his writing and he writes fiction for pleasure. He lives with his wife, two teenage children and a small collection of interesting vehicles: 'on the button' and ready for their next adventure!

William Philpott is a member of Rugby Cafe Writers.

Steve Redshaw was born and raised in Sussex. Over the past forty years he has taught young children in the South of England and East Anglia. He has now retired and is living aboard his narrowboat, Miss Amelia, on the Oxford Canal near Rugby. His passion is music, singing and playing guitar, and various other plucked instruments, in pubs, folk clubs and sessions around the area. He also is a dance caller for Barn Dances and Ceilidhs. His creative output is perhaps best described as emergent and sporadic, but when time allows, he enjoys composing songs and writing short stories.

Chris Rowe. Just before covid, Chris tried to write poetry: lockdown gave the time to attempt different poetic forms - even a sonnet. Her interests, in more agile days, were fell-walking and cross-country skiing, and Chris is currently a hard-put-upon housekeeper to a rescue cat. From childhood, Chris has been interested in reading prose: such as Richmal Crompton (*Just William*), Alison Utley (*Sam Pig*), Henry Fielding, Mark Twain, Jane Austen, and Terry Pratchett.

Shakespeare has always been a favourite and long ago the ambition was achieved of seeing a performance of every play: *Antony and Cleopatra* being the hardest to track down (all those scene changes deter production.). Favourite performers of the Bard are Oddsocks.

Linda Slate has lived in Rugby for 11 years. She has four children, 15 grandchildren and three great-grandchildren. She has worked as a teacher and a police officer, both jobs have given her inspiration for her writing. Along with swimming, writing has been a lifelong passion. She has not yet had a novel published, but hopes to have one ready to submit by the end of 2023.

Christopher Trezise was born and raised in Rugby and pursued a professional acting career on theatre stages culminating in work for Disneyland Paris. Christopher has held many jobs from kitchen assistant through to risk management consultant but he has always had a passion for writing. He runs several table-top roleplaying groups which he writes scenarios for and has self-published a fantasy book based upon one of those games.

Lindsay Woodward has had a lifelong passion for writing, starting off as a child when she used to write stories about the Fraggles of *Fraggle Rock*. Knowing there was nothing else she'd rather study, she did her degree in writing and has now turned her favourite hobby into a career. She writes from her home in Rugby, where she lives with her husband and cat. When she's not writing, Lindsay runs a Marketing Agency, where she spends most of her time copywriting, so words really are her life. Her debut novel, *Bird*, was published in April 2016, and Lindsay's 9th novel is due to be released in 2023.

Chris Wright says the following:
My earliest memory is of my mother using flashcards
to teach me to read while still in my playpen
we lived in a flat at West Heath,
a Vimto only area of Birmingham,
so my poetry is restricted
to about fifty different words
usually including "hippopotamus"

Printed in Great Britain
by Amazon

20172348R00092